PRAISE FOR MIDNIGHT WORSHIP

Dr. Preston Nix:

"In his book Midnight Worship, the author Drake Nelson uses 'midnight' as a metaphor for the worst problems in life that we cannot solve and the almost impossible situations in which we find ourselves that we cannot fix. Opening the book in dramatic fashion about a car wreck that he and his girlfriend miraculously survived, Drake shares compelling stories of personal struggles as well as riveting illustrations of the 'midnights' of people he has known along with Bible characters who learned to worship God in the midst of and in spite of the great difficulties in which they found themselves. Drake's stated purpose in the book is not to deal with the philosophical and theological question of why bad things happen to good people but to show believers how they can cope with and continue to keep their faith 'through the bad' they will encounter in this life. If you are facing a seemingly impossible situation and wondering how you are going to make it, read this very practical book and allow the Lord to use both the touching stories and the truth of Scripture to help you to continue to trust Him and worship Him through your personal 'midnight.'"

Sam Taylor:

"Midnight Worship is great reminder of how God's glory shines through even the darkest circumstances. It will encourage readers to seek and worship Jesus no matter what."

Dr. Blake Smith:

"In a world of much suffering, this book offers wisdom and encouragement in the midst of everyday struggles we experience in our lives. Nelson is able to captivate his audience by sharing some of his own personal 'midnights' which ignites a personal connection with many of his readers as they plunge into this journey of spiritual growth"

Midnight Worship

© 2020 by Drake Nelson

All rights reserved. No portion of this book may be reproduced, stored in a retrieval system, or transmitted in any form or by any means—electronic, mechanical, photocopy, recording, scanning, or other—without the prior written permission of the publisher, except in the case of brief quotations in critical reviews or articles.

Published in Brookhaven, Mississippi, by Epiphany House Publishing.

Scripture quotations marked NIV are taken from the New International Version, NIV. Copyright © 1973, 1978, 1984, 2011 by Biblica, Inc. Used by permission of Zondervan. All rights reserved worldwide. www.zondervan.com. The "NIV" and "New International Version" are trademarks registered in the United States Patent and Trademark Office by Biblica, Inc.

Scripture quotations marked ESV are taken from the ESV Bible (The Holy Bible, English Standard Version), copyright © 2001 by Crossway, a publishing ministry of Good News Publishers. Used by permission. All rights reserved.

Scripture quotations marked NKJV are taken from the New King James Version. © 1982 by Thomas Nelson. Used by permission. All rights reserved.

Scripture quotations marked KJV are taken from The King James Version of the Bible. © 1993, 1994, 1995, 1996, 2000. Used by permission of NavPress Publishing Group. All rights reserved.

Scripture quotations marked NLT are taken from the Holy bible, New Living Translation. © 1996, 2004, 2007, 2013 by Tyndale House Foundation. Used by permission of Tyndale House Publishers, Inc., Carol Stream, Illinois 60188. All rights reserved.

Library of Congress Control Number: 2019914872

ISBN 978-1-7340892-0-2 (paperback)
ISBN 978-1-7340892-1-9 (hardback)
ISBN 78-1-7340892-2-6 (eBook)

Printed in the United States of America

Acknowledgments:

Writing a book is harder than I ever thought it would be. *Midnight Worship* has been years in the making but none of it would have been possible without an amazing human being, Catherine Moultrie. You have always been patient while I have put our life on hold to write this book. I love you so much, and thank you for everything you do.

To my dear family, I want to say, "Thank you." You mean the world to me. To the parents who raised me, Tyson and Christy Nelson, "You are the best parents I could ask for." To my two brothers, Drew and Ty Nelson, who have taught me more than I could ever repay, "You guys are truly special. I am proud to call you my brothers but more importantly, my brothers in Christ. I love you." To my beautiful sister, Marley Sue Nelson, "You make me feel wanted, loved, cherished, and you have always been supportive of me through this journey called, life. I love you."

A very special thanks to my publishing team. You guys and girls rock! Shout out to Megan Matheney. You have been a tremendous help. I appreciate all your effort in making this book great. You are the best editor I could ask for. To Kris Sullivan, Janey Blakeney, and Kayla Sandifer (aka, KK ☺), "Thank you all so much for helping make this book happen."

I am eternally grateful to Blake Smith. Thank you for being an encouragement through the process of writing this book. Thank you to Roy Martin for helping with advertisement, and Jan Ratcliff for the fantastic book cover and formatting. Special thanks to Shelby Lang for taking marvelous book cover pictures.

Lastly, I want to thank Brandon and Whitney Warren. You guys are awesome and have helped me out in so many ways with life that I will never be able to repay. You are examples to Catherine and I on how to love each other and walk after Jesus. We love y'all!

CONTENTS

Introduction 9

Chapter One - Greater Than Your Midnight 19

Chapter Two - Midnight in Philippi 37

Chapter Three - The Key to Midnight 53

Interlude - Rooms of Unanswered Prayers 65

Chapter Four - Room of Death 69

Chapter Five - Gym of Dreams 93

Interlude - The Story Continues 117

Chapter Six - A Different Kind of Earthquake 121

Chapter Seven - Room of Mental—or
Not-so-Mental Health 135

Chapter Eight - Room of Vulnerability 153

Chapter Nine - Full Moon Christian 181

Chapter Ten - Room of Relationships 197

Chapter Eleven - Noonday and Sunburnt 233

Chapter Twelve - Room of Our Past 253

Chapter Thirteen - The Proposal 269

End Notes 282

INTRODUCTION

9-1-1

I remember waking up to a throbbing headache. My first thought was directed towards asking Catherine if she was hurt.

As I looked over, still trying to regain my memory, Catherine responded with a simple, "I'm okay. Are you?"

"Nuh uh," I muttered before blacking out again.

Waking up a second time to Catherine pulling me out of the driver's seat, I immediately knew something was wrong. In the first place, I couldn't remember how I ended up on the ground.

I quickly did a self-check to make sure all my systems would operate. Toes, check. Legs, check. Knees, check. Arms and neck, check. Back, check.

After I frantically rubbed my hand back and forth over my head to see if I was bleeding (which luckily, I wasn't), I did what every twenty-one-year-old does in times of frantic: call Mom.

"Hello" she answered. The tone of my voice was different than it had ever been. It was somehow solemn yet concerned.

The first thought I wanted to communicate was that I was okay.

"Hey, Mom. Don't panic, but I was in a wreck. I think it was a bad one, but I'm okay. My back is hurting, but I can move. An ambulance is on its way to get us."

"Us ... who is us?" Mom retorted.

"Me and my girlfriend; she was in the car with me. She is okay too." (Later on in the week, Mom confessed that her first line of thinking was *"Drake has a girlfriend?"*)

Not being able to muster up enough words because of the difficulty conversing with a broken neck, I handed the phone over to Catherine who introduced herself and explained everything that happened.

(We had flipped a 2006 soft-top convertible into a stranger's field.)

Meanwhile, the paramedics arrived on the scene a few minutes after the phone call and confirmed that my neck was probably broken. The good news was that I had full range of motion, which meant my spinal cord was not severed.

The paramedics proceeded to put me in a body suit which I thought was cool because I looked like Iron Man. So there I sat, waiting for the ambulance to arrive.

I had no idea what was going on around me. I couldn't move my head due to the neck brace I was in.

I began to count the different voices I heard: one, two, three, four. There were at least ten people there. I wanted to thank them, but I couldn't speak loud enough for anyone to hear.

Catherine began to pick up the clothes that were scattered from the wreck. I practically lived in my vehicle, so the farmer's field looked like a flea market. There was everything from tennis rackets to clothes, from books to fishing poles, all scattered amongst what used to be corn stalks.

It was in the late fall when the wreck happened—November 7th to be exact—and that morning was brutally chilly with a cold front blowing over from Louisiana.

As Catherine was trying to find something warm to wear, the ambulance finally arrived.

Putting me on a stretcher, the paramedics carried me to Yazoo Baptist Hospital. I was placed in a luxurious half-room with a curtain separating me from a heart-attack patient. As if that wasn't surreal enough, their only doctor was out sick, the nurse practitioner was taking vacation, my parents were still two hours away, and the nurses had to tend to the guy on my left dying of a myocardial infarction. So there I sat—alone.

I had felt alone before but not like this. This was different. I actually needed someone there.

What felt like hours passed, until I began to vomit all over the room. (I quickly realized that if you ever want attention in a hospital, just start vomiting on walls and someone will quickly come to your aid.)

The nurses came in and took care of me the best they knew how. And when I say the best they knew how, I mean they did nothing but inform me, "You're going to be okay sweetheart. We are so sorry. Are you okay? Awe, poor baby."

That is no vilification of the nurses. My nurses were amazing, but after getting a concussion and before getting a CAT scan, there is little that can medically be done. (As a side note, I just want to say that eventually, to cause me not to aspirate, the nurses had to turn my stretcher on its side. It was in that moment, sideways on a stretcher and vomiting on the walls, that my parents first walked in.)

Knock, knock, we heard at the door. The head nurse eased her way in: "That was quite some accident you had, young man. You are lucky to be alive." Nodding as to indicate agreement, she began to wheel me back to the CAT machine. While I was gone, Catherine began to show signs of a concussion as well.

Due to the lack of doctors, I was sent by ambulance to the University of Mississippi Medical Center, the largest hospital in Mississippi.

As I was being pushed out on the stretcher, I heard a conversation going on just outside my room. It was a bunch of whispering, and I knew whispering in a hospital couldn't be a good sign.

Mom caught a glimpse of me as I was being rolled down the hall, so she ran down to catch me before I left. I was freaking out because this was one of the only times I had ever seen Mom run. She was blunt about it and with tears in her eyes she told me the news: Catherine had two brain bleeds and might not make it.

My gurney never stopped rolling. They rolled me up into the ambulance and off I went—not knowing what was to come of Catherine.

Hot tears began to roll down my cheeks. The whole time I was worried about myself when I should have been worrying about Catherine.

Somehow, the EMT found out that I was a youth pastor, so he started asking me all these questions about God. I did my best to answer him, and in that moment, the story of Jesus came to mind. About how in the hardest times of his life, he had the faith to look at the guy on his side and minister to him. I did my best to replicate that. We would reconnect later. However, that is another story for another time.

As I arrived at UMMC, the doctors had good news for me. The CAT scan showed I had no internal bleeding, and no broken neck, just a fractured upper back and a concussion. (While I am writing this, I am on the beach and it has been about six months since the wreck, but I can still feel exactly where my back got bent out of shape—literally ☺. I am about to get one of my brothers to walk on it. Hopefully it will feel better. Long day of boogie boarding ahead for me tomorrow.)

But the good news quickly turned into oceans of frustration. UMMC called a helicopter to come and airlift Catherine to the hospital, but due to storms in the area, it was not able to land. As a last resort, she was rushed by ambulance to UMMC, and as she arrived, the trauma team greeted her and prepped Catherine for surgery. In all, there were somewhere between twelve and fifteen doctors surrounding her. Before I knew it, she was being wheeled away, leaving me to wonder if I would ever get to see her again.

I will talk more about this story later, but that was the worst day of my twenty-one years on Earth—but I am aware that some of you live in days much worse than that. You are in a place right now where there seems to be no way out. It seems as if life will never go back to the way it was. Your plans did not work out. You have lost all hope and worth in life. You have backed yourself into a corner and don't know how to get out.

> Build the shelter in the sun, so that when the storm comes, you can stay dry.

Maybe you got a call from the doctor and only have three months to live. Maybe you lost the love of your life because of a decision that was rationed by you. Maybe your marriage is sinking into deep waters. Or maybe you are in a hole of financial debt but can barely hold your head above the water.

INTRO

Maybe you have lost a child, lost a job, lost a loved one, lost a friend, lost your money, lost your mind, lost your way, lost three years of your life, lost faith, lost hope, or maybe you have even lost yourself. But I can tell you this, "God leaves the ninety-nine sheep to find the one that's lost." No matter how dark the night, God is not done with you.

If you're reading this book and you are not in a dark night right now—it's lunch time on the beach and you're chilling with your kiddos; life is overall going well—this book is for you. Build the shelter in the sun, so that when the storm comes, you can stay dry.

In 2005 the worst storm to hit this nation, Hurricane Katrina, ended up in my backyard. We knew it was coming a few days beforehand, so we bought plenty of water, a generator, twenty gallons of gas, flashlights, candles, canned foods, a chainsaw, and anything else you may need to weather a bad storm. And so, we were ready. After the storm passed, our power stayed out for two weeks. Because we were prepared, we not only provided food and water for ourselves, but for our neighbors and to those who were coming up from New Orleans. Life can sometimes throw things at the worst moments, but if we're expecting it and have a game plan, it's always easier to handle. I can tell you this: If you are on your lunch break right now and life is good, there will come a time when the lights go dark. If you are prepared, you can provide shelter not only for yourself, but for those around you and for those who are evacuating their storms in search of a shelter.

If you're reading this book in the midst of the dark night and are so angry with God for what he has put you through—you are thinking about giving up on God because he has given up on you—this book is for you.

Although I cannot say why we go through tragedy, dark nights, or storms, I know that God is with us through it all. He doesn't promise that we won't go through it, but he does promise to walk through the dark with us.

I have grown up with awful knees. I had my first knee surgery when I was thirteen. A few years later, I had an ACL and MCL replacement. Each morning after the surgery when I came into physical therapy, my therapist, Jack, would see how far I could bend my knee. Our goal was to attain ten degrees more bend over the stretch of nine weeks. The weeks were easy until week eight. No matter how hard I tried or how much therapy I did, I could not get my knee to straighten or bend completely. Jack explained to me that it wasn't a lack of muscle that hindered me from bending my knee, but a buildup of scar tissue between my joints from the surgery. (This apparently is a common thing in many surgeries.)

I asked Jack if I would ever be able to have full range of motion in my knee again, and with a grin, he said, "Oh yeah."

He sat me down on the couch/table thing they had in the P.T. room. As I laid there, he brought me a towel to bite down on and water to drink. I knew then that I was in for a treat. He then grabbed a giant rolling rod that was about three foot in length and an inch thick with hard, plastic circles covering the outside.

As I laid there, he rolled that rod over my knee using all his weight, and I could feel the scar tissue breaking in my knee. I screamed and tried to move, but his assistants held me down. I'll never forget the prophetic words he spoke to me in that moment: "I know it hurts Drake, but breaking this scar tissue is the only way to walk again." Those words pierced my soul.

Even though I may not understand why God allowed me to tear my ACL, I knew that God had my best interest at heart.

I can't tell you why you are going through what you are going through, but I can tell you that God has your best interest at heart, and sometimes he must break you in order for you to walk again.

Enough of me speaking about God and for God; you speak to God. Ask him why you are going through your storm. Ask him why your life is the way it is and listen for an answer. I believe God is a communicator. He will come find us. Maybe you won't hear from God now but be persistent in asking and keep an open ear. I believe he will give you an answer.

Right here I want to stop and say for those of you who are done with God, done with Church, hate the dark night that you're in, and will not waste anymore of your time reading this, please do not throw this book away. Maybe your life is amazing, and you do not see any point in reading a book about midnight when you are in noonday. I just ask, please don't throw this book away. Put it in a dresser, in a closet, in your vehicle, on your bookshelf, somewhere that you can find it again one day. Maybe in ten years, ten months, or ten weeks, you will find yourself needing to read. And who knows, you might just take it out, pick it up, and read it. (If it's been like ten years and you're just now reading it, please tell me that Apple has invented an all glass phone.)

If you have been beat down, run down, bruised up, stepped on, disregarded, disrespected, unwanted, unloved, unhappy, unapologetic, runover, run-away, run-through, or are simply running out of hope, this book is for you.

We are going to contemplate how, during the hardest moments of our life, the hardest thing to do can be to worship God. But how through worshiping God, life and restoration can be brought back. Your life isn't over.

Let's Go!!

CHAPTER ONE

GREATER THAN YOUR MIDNIGHT

My eyes are as dry as my soul. No more tears can formulate, but deep within my soul arises oceans of frustration. I am being wheeled back to my room as the doctors sprint past me—their white coats seemingly floating. I am of no ill will towards God or any other entity outside of my own control, but the vexations with myself are endless. A hospital is a good place to feel sad.

Will she ever walk out of here?
How can I overcome it if she doesn't?
She hasn't even turned twenty-one yet.

Her parents have not arrived at UMMC yet, nor am I allowed to walk in to check on her. Earlier, as Catherine's gurney passed mine, the gentle touch of fingertips could be our last embrace. Was that really how the LORD allowed me to say, "Goodbye?" After all, not many people make it out of a surgery of this magnitude.

I gently push my tongue against the nearside of my teeth. I read somewhere doing this releases tension.

Catherine has the prettiest smile, baby-blue eyes, strawberry blonde hair, a beautiful complexion. We just met a few weeks ago, and now look at us! The sound of panic floods the Trauma Unit. The little red car will not flee from my memory bank. Over and over again, I watch the wreck unfold, helpless to stop it.

Two large dark spots revealed by an MRI scan are the rationale behind all the panic. Brain bleeds kill!

A song arises and from it, more questions articulate in my mind—Elevation Worship's "Do it Again." Feeling anything but full of faith, I will choose to believe again. Right here in this moment of confusion, I will lift my praise. Scriptures I memorized as a child resurface, and I am so proud for the lesson. I am afraid. But I am not alone. This is *Midnight Worship*.

WHAT COULD YOUR MIDNIGHT BE?

For some of you, when you saw the title of this book you knew precisely what your midnight was. You didn't even have to think about it because you face it every day. Others of you may not know what your midnight is or that you are even going through one. Either way, it is helpful to articulate what kind of midnights can do us the most harm.[i]

- Maybe your midnight is *death*. Someone close to you passed away unexpectedly, and you didn't get the chance to tell them everything

you wanted. Alternatively, maybe the death was expected, but the pain was not.
- Maybe the midnight of *relationships* has sunk its teeth into you. Someone told you they would never leave and would always love you, only to break your heart.
- Maybe you had a *change of plans*. You are not where you thought you would be. The job that you were counting on fell through. You did not get into the college you dreamed of. Maybe the product that you were pushing did not do as well as you hoped it would.
- Maybe your midnight is your *past*. You have made some colossal mistakes and are now suffering the consequences. It could be something that you did. Or worse, something that was done to you.

EMBERS OF WORSHIP

A few months before the wreck, I had a bird that kept coming to my window night after night, keeping me awake with constant chirping. After about the fifth night, I got up with every intention to put an end to this chirping once and for all. I grabbed my pellet gun, found some slippers, and walked out the back door. Creeping around the carport to the gravel driveway, a light pole lit up the front yard just enough for me to discover my feathered little friend was a mockingbird.

After reading *To Kill a Mockingbird* in high school, I grew fond of them. So, instead of killing it, I went back inside, turned on my box fan, and tried to get some sleep.

The chirping continued the next night and the next and the next until, eventually, I became accustomed to the sound. I also became curious as to why all of a sudden this mockingbird began to chirp during the early summer nights.

I did some research on it, also known as Google, and discovered a fascinating article in the Los Angeles Times that included this statement: "Mockingbirds sing at the midnight hour, not out of joy, but out of desperation."[ii]

It was this idea that sparked the embers of *Midnight Worship* for me. I wanted to become like this mockingbird, able to offer praises to God while in the desperation of midnight.

But how?

And Could I?

MY MIDNIGHT

Looking back, my midnight came from two things: the inability to ask for help and perfectionism.

Growing up, I was asked by my parents to do everything. Each day I would come home from school and hear, "Drake, can you bring me a glass of Diet Dr. Pepper?" "Drake, can you bring me the T.V. remote?" "Drake, can you wash my vehicle?" I became the household servant. Now my parents are not lazy at all. In fact, they are the hardest-working people I know. But in my early days of childhood, it didn't matter if I had friends over, a baseball game that night, or a test to study for; whatever needed to be done, I got stuck doing it. I usually didn't mind doing these chores. To be honest, I was glad to help out in any way that I could. Now I know what you may be thinking, *"This is some lazy punk writing."* Maybe so, but over time I grew a resentment towards asking anyone for help.

Coupled with that, I am a perfectionist. I am a perfectionist in the smallest of tasks such as organizing my desk drawer, and also in the largest of endeavors like writing this book. I cannot tell you how many times I have written words down, thought they were great, and then erased them because I thought I could do better. On the surface, being a perfectionist may appear to be a good thing—and it can be. But when left unmonitored, perfectionism leads into a dark place.

These are the two character flaws that led to my midnight. They came prancing into my life dressed as nobility, so I thought they were noble. But I soon found this to be a lie. In actuality, they were the bricks that paved a road that I did not want to walk down.

Not everyone struggles with perfectionism and the inability to ask for help. Some of you may struggle with unforgiveness, loneliness, or addiction. Still others may struggle with their self-image. Maybe those aren't your bricks. But whatever they are, it is vital that you come to recognize the hazards walking you down the road to midnight.

Perfectionism and not asking anyone for help were perceived by me to be good. I may have even said beneficial. Turns out, I was wrong. Facing these giants came with a self-inflicting pain because I hated to ask anyone for help—so I didn't—and I wanted to prove to myself that I was "okay" (that was the perfectionist in me speaking). Perfectionism and helplessness were not scoundrels that sent me into a hole of anxiety, depression, grief, or heartache. No, they simply kept me from the things that God intended—namely, comradery and wisdom. The same is true for you! Not every midnight has to come on the backside of heartbreak and loss. Midnights are not always misery, depression, hopelessness, and despair. Sometimes they might be, but midnights *are and begin* any time we have less than God's best in our lives.

> **Midnights are and begin any time we have less than God's best in our lives.**

WHAT IS YOUR REBAR?

It wasn't until my first year of graduate school that I began to learn the significance of rebar. I was headed to New Orleans on I-55 when a car dashed off the road and into the bridge parapet. I had often wondered what would happen if a car ran into one of those, but I found out firsthand. The concrete fissured, and the car went sideways. Luckily, the rebar kept everything and everyone from running off the bridge. *What a terrible way to have started the morning— an early morning dip into the Pontchartrain.*

I went home after the accident and looked up why rebar was so essential to concrete. The simple answer is, concrete is high on compressive strength but low in tensile strength, whereas steel provides high tensile strength which is lacking in concrete. So, to balance what concrete lacks, rebar is added. It reinforces the concrete.[iii]

To which you're thinking, *"English, please."* Basically, rebar holds the concrete together. And that is exactly what worship does in our lives. It holds us together in times of trouble. It binds us through trials and difficulties. It allows us to bring out our inner diamond when pressure is added. I have heard it said, "No pain, no gain." But I like to say, "No pain, no pain." I don't want despair to thunder into my life and neither do you, but when it does, worship is the rebar which will hold us together.

I will refer to Louie Giglio often throughout this book because he has been a role model in my life. He defines *worship* as a shift that allows us to see God better.[iv]

Think about that statement; *a shift that allows us to better see God.* In the darkest moments of life, it can be hard to see anything—especially God's purpose and plan through it all.

Many authors have tried to tackle the age-old question, "How does a good God allow bad things to happen?"

Books such as *The Problem of Pain* by C.S. Lewis; *God, Freedom, and Evil* by Alvin Plantinga; and *Why Suffering* by Ravi Zacharias and Vince Vitale have been written to help with one's understanding of this topic. **However, it is not my purpose through these pages to answer why bad things happen, but rather to address how we keep our faith in God through the bad.**

Once when I was younger, I got lost in the woods coming back from deer hunting. I was only a child, so once the sun went down, I had no idea what to do. I sat there with my flashlight for what felt like an hour until, eventually, I began to shout as loud as I could, "*Daddddddddyyyyy, Dadddddddyyyyy.*" I cried and screamed, probably for thirty minutes, until I saw a light coming through the woods. And, at last, Dad was there to rescue me.

My hope is that this book will do the same for you. That it will give you a game plan on how to handle yourself in the night until your heavenly father comes to your rescue. Before we dive into the text of Acts 16, ask God to speak with you. Go ahead. Ask him. Don't get cold feet. Put down the book and ask God if he would speak into your life through these pages and begin something new. What are you waiting for?

HOW DOES YOUR VOICE SOUND?

Paul ducked his head as he shuffled outside his tent. Luke, Timothy, and Silas joined him on his journey.

His breakfast settled uneasy as the smell of fire spread through Lydia's home. She was considered the best tradesman in all of Philippi.

"How much time before we can go to the Synagogue?" Paul asked.

"Just a few more minutes! Let me finish up breakfast."

A slave girl who could tell the future accompanied them on their journey. As they arrived, she began to shout, "These men are servants of the Most High God, and they have come to tell us how to be saved." (Acts 16:17, NLT)

Day after day, this slave girl shouted the same thing until Paul became so exasperated that he turned and said to the demon within her, "I command you in the name of Jesus Christ, 'come out of her.'"

Maybe you are like me and wonder why the girl shouting, "These are the servants of the Most High God," aggravated Paul so much? I think for a few reasons: namely the persistence of her shouting.

If you are a mom, just imagine your little boy following you around all day yelling, "Mom, mom, mom, mom, mom, mom, mom." After about the thirty-seventh "mom", you're going to turn around and put duct tape over little Johnny's mouth. (By the way, I never knew duct tape was spelled with a *t*. I always thought it was duck tape. You learn something new every day I guess.)

The more important question that arises for me is, *"Why wait days while this girl is shouting in your ear, to cast the demon out of her? Why not just do it on the first day?"*

I think it was because Paul knew some things.

- He knew that he had a mission from God.
- He knew there were people to reach, churches to plant, and people to encourage.
- He knew there were broken families that needed to be mended.
- He knew before he started his prison ministry, he had a public ministry to engage in first. So that girl—as annoying as she was—had to wait.

Can you relate? Perhaps the girl screaming in your ear is a pile of bills that need to be paid, your children acting out, depression that is sinking its teeth into you, a relationship that has not gone the way you anticipated, a business partner that has stabbed you in the back, a family member who is casting down your every move and giving you no hope for the future that you want for yourself. Perhaps it is a lifetime of bad decisions.

Maybe the girl yelling in your ear day after day is a literal voice: your spouse. Perhaps your marriage is on the brink, and you see no way out besides signing the divorce papers. Maybe the girl yelling in your ear is no girl at all, but Satan himself. He is telling you how worthless you are and that no one cares about you or sees you. Whomever the girl that's shouting in your ear is, I want to show you her true identity: A SLAVE.

The voice screaming in your ear day after day is a slave to Jesus, under his control, and in his command.

When Jesus died, he ended sin's rule over us, fear's grip on us, and deaths power in us.

Now you may be thinking, *"I have been telling the voice antagonizing me to stop for months. I have been praying about it. I have talked to my friends about it. I have read books on it. I have even talked to my pastor, but I can still hear the voice, and it is as loud as ever."*

If you are there right now, I want to offer you some encouragement; *you are not alone.* Many people feel that. Paul felt that. David felt that. Jesus felt that. But in life, there are seasons for everything, even a season for voices. Ecclesiastes 3 tells us as much— "For everything there is a season." There may be a time when God lets a voice shout in your ear, but know this: Jesus is in control and sovereign over it all. He is greater than every slave, every sin, and every midnight that comes into your life.

Over the next few chapters, we're going to look at a variety of common and harmful midnights—trials that look unconquerable and hopeless. And we're going to see your deliverance from these midnights. But you're not going to be left standing alone with the mantra, "you can get over it if you try harder." You're going to meet a savior who walks into your story and into your midnight with you, lifts you up on his shoulder, and carries you to a place on high ground; a place of safety; a place of worship.

Name Above All Names

Two years ago, I was listening to a sermon at the Lift Tour by Louie, and he gave an interesting take on the David and Goliath story. He was speaking from his book, *Goliath Must Fall*, and painted a picture so beautifully as he spoke to deliver his final point. I want to try to recapture some of the main points of his story, beginning with David walking into the camp.

As he came into the valley of Elah to drop some food off for his brothers, David heard it: the voice of Goliath shouting in the background. Hearing the murmuring of fear around the camp, David went to approach Saul. "I'll go defeat this Philistine. I mean, who does he think he is anyhow? Can he get away with defying the armies of God?" Saul laughed, but David persisted, "No, for real. Once, when I was tending my father's sheep—oh yeah, dad makes me watch over his silly sheep because I am the youngest—not the greatest job. Anyways, when I was watching the sheep one day, a lion came and grabbed a lamb and guess what I did? I took my club and beat that thing to death. Then some bear decided it wanted to do the same thing, so I beat the hair off of it too. Yep, killed them both, and I'll kill this Philistine in the same way. There is going to be no funeral today. Well, there will be one, but not for us. For that stupid giant over there shouting too loud." Finally, Saul decided to give David a shot. "You got a bear and a lion under your belt. That's a pretty good résumé. After all, nobody else is offering to go."

As David walked down to the stream running into the middle of the valley, he grabbed a few stones. Then he headed towards Goliath. When Goliath saw him, he chuckled, "Silly boy, I am going to make you buzzard food." However, David smiled back replying, "Today, you come at me with a sword, a spear, and a javelin, but I come at you with a name, the name of God" (1 Samuel 17:45; authors paraphrase).

At that moment, David could have said, "Dude, I am coming against you with this slingshot I got from Saul, and, just to let you know, back home they call me 'Sniper Slingshot.' I just picked up five stones out of the brook and they're smooth so they will curve just enough to where you won't even see them coming. To be honest, I don't even know why I gathered five. I only need one because I am about to take you down son." But David didn't say that, did he? Instead, he came up to Goliath and said, "Yep, you are going to die. Not by this slingshot or these stones, but by a name. I have the name of God, and he is on my side, and you are going to die."

To translate that to our conversation today is to simply say a couple of things. The first point is this: get your five stones if you need them. In other words, *it's okay to get help; in fact, if you need help, get help.* If you need to get on medication, please, by all means, get on medication. If you need to go to therapy, go and get counseling. If you need government assistance, please sign up for it. The reason that medication, therapy, and government assistance exist is to help people who need it. But when it's all said and done, it's not the medicine or the therapy or the handout that is going to get you through the midnight. It is the name of Jesus.

The name of Jesus has power.

We are not looking at the midnight and putting our confidence in a pill, a paycheck, or a person. No, instead we are looking at the midnight and declaring, "I have a name that is above every name, and that name will carry me through." How is it possible that we can defeat our enemies and find deliverance with a name? *Because the name of Jesus has power.*

A few years ago, when I was in my first year of college, a campus police officer knocked on the window of my car to inform me that he had called a tow truck to remove my car from the premises. Apparently, I wasn't parked in a parking space.

To be honest, I really wasn't, but if you're a college student, you can empathize with me because trying to find somewhere to park is equivalent to mission impossible.

In hindsight, it was probably not the smartest response, but I got out of the car and informed Mr. Police Officer that he must have lost his mind if he thought I was going to let him tow my vehicle. Well boys and girls, that was the wrong thing for me to say. Next thing I knew, he was putting me in the back of his cop car and threatening to take me to jail. Well, by this time I was furious. I grabbed my phone and began to call my tennis coach, who also happened to be the dean of school.

"Whom do you need to call at a time like this kid?" the police officer muttered. "Oh nobody, just your boss. Oh yeah, who, by the way, is my tennis coach. And don't think I am not going to tell her exactly how this conversation went down and how you treated me. To the very last detail," I retorted. Well, to make a short story even shorter, about two minutes later he apologized, helped me out of the car, and told me to find a better place to park next time. But why? Because a name carries power with it. The name of Jesus is greater than any valley you will walk through, any giant you will face, and any midnight that comes your way. The name of Jesus WILL get you through any and every circumstance.

I don't know if you are aware of the song or not, but Michael W. Smith came out with a song called "Surrounded" in 2018. There are only three lines in the entire song, but it goes something like this; "This (being worship) is how I fight my battles, this is how I fight my battles, this is how I fight my battles." The song says that line over and over until it eventually switches to the verse "When it looks like I'm surrounded, I'm surrounded by you. When it looks like I'm surrounded, I'm surrounded by you."

That song pretty much sums up this entire chapter and, to be honest, is a metanarrative of this book. Worship is how we fight against every battle we face, and it is how we walk through any midnight that we find ourselves in. When it seems like we are surrounded by our enemies, our self-doubt, or our circumstance, our God surrounds us in those very moments. Our God surrounds the very thing that seems to be surrounding us.

As pastor Louie finished up his sermon, he famously said: "We are not David in the Story of David and Goliath. Jesus is David in the story of David and Goliath."[v]

It's not really about us mustering up enough faith and courage that keeps Jesus fresh on our lips and in our prayers, rather it's understanding that Jesus is the one who will carry us through any and every midnight that we walk through.[vi]

MW

CHAPTER TWO

MIDNIGHT IN PHILIPPI

Cowering as a fist hurled towards his face, Paul began to backstep as the owners of the slave girl closed in on him and Silas.

Silas spoke up, "Okay guys, let's not get too upset. After all, we helped cure this girl of a demon. Sooooooo, you should be thanking us—right?"

Paul noticed he was grinding his teeth in angst as the owners grabbed both him and Silas.

Making eye contact with the **ruffian dragging** him by his collar sent another fist jolting towards his face—this time making contact with his right eye.

"Silas," Paul said in a soft voice.

"Yes, I am here."

"Where are we? I can't see."

"I think we are in the marketplace. There is a guard to our left watching us, and the owners are over to our right talking to what looks like the city officials." Silas continued, "Listen. I think I can hear what they are saying."

"These men are teaching things that are illegal for us Romans!" the owners belted. "And because of it, the entire city is in an uproar. These men," they said, pointing to Paul and Silas, "have ruined our business. They are the reason for all this commotion. They are leaders of an insurrection; one of a new king. One not of Rome."

The crowd soon became enraged. "Kill them, kill them, kill them."

Roman soldiers came quickly for Paul and Silas and carried them to be beaten. They stripped them of their clothes, and the beating proceeded. The crowd followed, and after a few shots to the rib cage, Paul cried out in pain, causing the mob to roar even louder.

A few minutes after the beating ceased, the swell of noise subsided.

"Is it over?" asked Silas.

"Yes, I think so. Are you okay?"

"I don't know. I can't feel anything."

"Let's go, boys," the soldiers said. "We're taking you both to prison."

By this time, Paul's face had become completely unrecognizable. He was so beaten and battered that he hardly appeared human. The jailer came out to be introduced to his new inmates. (He routinely needn't have taken such elaborate measures, except that he knew his life depended on these prisoners not escaping.) He carried the half-dead men to the inner part of the prison while the lesser aides came in to bind their feet in clamps.

MIDNIGHT IN PHILIPPI

The cold chains of the prison floor had become familiar to Paul, but not yet for Silas. Silas was angry—"Why do they hate us so much, Paul? If this is what we get for doing the right thing, then what is justice? And if this is what the Lord gives to those who do his work, why even call him Lord?"

Breathing deeply, wheezing as he exhaled, Paul began to sing in a soft voice:

> *"God, you're so good,*
> *God, you're so good,*
> *God, you're so good,*
> *You're so good, to meeee."*

Silas, spitting up some blood and still offended by his unfair treatment, conceded to join in:

> *"Lord I need you,*
> *Oh, I need you.*
> *Every hour I need you.*
> *My one defense,*
> *My righteousness,*
> *Oh God, how I need you."*

Their worship was interrupted by the clock as it struck midnight. The other prisoners were wide awake—shocked at what they were hearing. They looked around at each other with baffled looks as if to say, "These men have been beaten so badly, they have lost their minds. We are in prison. Why are you two worshiping God?"

After the clock finished its announcement of the new day, Paul and Silas lifted their voiced once again to Heaven:

> "When the night is holding on to me,
> God is holding on.
> When the night is holding on to me,
> God is holding on.
> 'Cause you are good,
> Good,
> Ohhhhhhhh, good.
> 'Cause you are good,
> Good,
> Ohhhhhh, good."

PURPOSE IN THE PRISON

Plenty of us find ourselves in similar predicaments. Although we may not face a literal prison, we are facing some sort of insurmountable challenge or difficulty that rips into our lives. Maybe its anxiety. Maybe its anger. Maybe its laziness. Maybe it's our past. Maybe it's the way we treat people. **Maybe it's the baggage that we tote around.**[i]

Our first response to being thrown into prison is to get out. That is our natural human tendency, but God's tendency is often to use us in spite of it—better yet, to use us through it.

Think about it. All Paul wanted to do was preach the Gospel to those who had never heard it before. He gave up everything he had for one mission, the Great Commission. And when he got his chance to share the Gospel, what happened? He was thrown into prison and chained to the floor.

One thing is for sure, Paul had greater faith than me. If it were me chained to the floor, I would have lamented, "God, all I want to do is preach, and you're going to let me be tied down, put in prison, and beaten? Why, God? I have given you my life. I don't understand this. It's not fair! Do you see me? Do you care? Do you have a plan in all this? Where are you, God?"

But Paul didn't say any of that. Instead, during his many years expended in prison, he became a prolific writer to the churches he had previously visited. Paul wrote to people like Philemon and Timothy, aiming to encourage them. He penned six books while he was incarcerated and, today, more people have been touched by those six books than Paul could have reached in a hundred years of public ministry. But how? Because God had bigger plans. It turns out that God knew what he was doing after all.

See, the central concept to understand when we are in prison is not God's purpose in it, but our purpose in life.

We can drive ourselves mad trying to find God's purpose in everything. In fact, you probably know someone who has given up on God because (s)he couldn't see God's incentive in the midst of tragedy.

If our purpose is to simply understand God's plan, we will be deflated when we can't see it. On the contrary, if our purpose is lifted above the prison and the tragedy, no power in Hell will be able to prevail against us.

I was trying to think of an example to illustrate this point, so I called up my eleventh-grade history teacher, Coach Craig Davis, and asked him for an example. When I called, he was hitting golf balls in his backyard ☺. He thought briefly, and soon said, "Okay Drake, I got you someone. Young Desmond Doss."

They made a movie on the veteran medic, Desmond, called *Hacksaw Ridge* so I'm not going to rehash his story, but when Desmond entered into WWII, he did not know God's purpose for battle or understand God's purpose in all the killing. However, Desmond knew his purpose in life. He lived in what some described as *Hell on Earth*, but in the midst of it all, he was able to offer relief to others who were in pain. He was able to save the lives of those who persecuted him months before. Desmond saw through the *midnight* and into something larger—and my friends, we have the opportunity to do the same.

Look at Paul's words as he writes from prison:

"Now I want you to know, brothers, that what has happened to me has really served to advance the Gospel. As a result, it has become clear throughout the whole palace guard and to everyone else that I am in chains for Christ" (Philippians 1:12-13, NIV).

So, have Kingdom eyes—be able to see beyond the pain and to the people because no matter your prison, you have a purpose.

We are called to go into battle, encounter people there, and help carry them out.

Why?

> No matter your prison, you have a purpose.

Because we have a Savior who arrived in our battle, carried us over his shoulder, and became our victory.

POWERFUL PURPOSE

Now you may ask, "How am I supposed to figure out my purpose in life? Is there any way you can help me find it, Drake?"

Yes, I believe I can. I am here for you!

First, let me ask a question: What is the bigger miracle? For God to deliver you from the pain, or for God to give you strength to persevere through it? Is it more miraculous for God to deliver you from going into the lions' den or for him to shut the mouths of the lions while you're in their cave?

To me, the bigger miracle is not for God to always offer deliverance out of the pain or out of the situation, but for God to be enough to support me in the midst of it—so that I can dispatch on the other side and be able to say, "I didn't like it. I don't want to walk through it again. But through it all, I never quit on God. I never gave up on him. Yeah, there were times when I had questions, but I kept my faith through it."

Rather God heals or doesn't will not affect the way I worship because I don't worship God for what he does but for who he is.

So, pray for God to take you out of the prison—yes, that is a good thing. But more importantly, I think, is to pray for the strength you need to be maintained through it.

Look at Paul. He did not ask others to pray that he was released from prison, but to be given boldness and courage while in it:

"And pray for me, too. Ask God to give me the right words so I can boldly explain God's mysterious plan that the Good News is for Jews and Gentiles alike. I am in chains now, still preaching this message as God's ambassador. So, pray that I will keep on speaking boldly for him, as I should" (Ephesians 6:19-20, NLT).

I do not want hard times to crash into my life. Neither did Paul and neither do you. But there is only one thing that will maintain us through it all, and that is a God-sized purpose. Therefore, what is our God-sized purpose?

The answer comes from 1 Corinthians 10:31: "So whether you eat or drink, or _**whatever you do, do it all for the glory of God**_" (1 Cor. 10:31; NLT).

And this is our purpose in life—to bring glory to God. Whether that is through teaching a classroom,

> "Whoever offers praises glorifies me."

preaching a sermon, playing a sport, parenting a child, or being an expert of law or medicine.

Whether that is by walking through the midnight, losing a loved one, being handcuffed to the prison floor, or being drafted into World War III, we are to do **_Everything_** to bring God glory. In other words, the ultimate goal of our lives is to glorify God.

Two significant questions often jam up peoples' lives at about the age of nineteen: "Who am I?" and "Why am I here?" The sad thing is that by the age of forty-two, people are still struggling to find their answers.

Isaiah 43:7 says we were made to glorify God. Psalms 19 asserts that all creation was made to glorify him. The New Testament comes around to affirm this in Colossians 1:16: "For all things were created through him *(talking about Jesus)* and for him."

So, worry no more about what your purpose is—**it is to glorify God.** But the question that still remains is, *How do we do that?*

Honestly, there are a multitude of ways, but the indispensable crux for us to bring glory to God is through our worship.

The Bible says it this way: "Whoever offers praises glorifies me" (Psalm 50:23, NKJV). I feel like I need to come alongside this idea and say that worship is so much more than singing a song; it is a way of life (See Hebrews 13:15).

A few years ago, I had a friend who could have been a model for Ralph Lauren. He was, and still is for that matter, a very handsome guy. But one day he began to lose his hair until, eventually, he went bald. That same friend called me a few days ago and told me he was depressed. His purpose and meaning in life were caught up in his appearance, but when that was diminished in his perspective, he felt that he had nothing.

I had another friend growing up whose parents were millionaires. Or so we thought. She lacked nothing growing up—the most expensive wardrobe, a Cadillac when she turned sixteen, the newest iPhone. But one day her family went bankrupt and had to sell everything. A few years later, she opened up and described how her purpose hinged on what she had. When everything was taken, her identity was, also.

I had a family member who committed suicide because his girlfriend broke up with him. But why? Because his meaning in life was defined by her, and when she left, he thought it would be better if he was dead.

When our purpose is in something other than God's glory, we will fail in the hardest of times. Notice that I say purpose and not faith. You can have faith in God without purpose, and then face trials and tribulations and lose your faith. You can then justify it to yourself by asking, *How could a loving God cause this to happen?*

If our purpose is in anything besides glorifying God,

which in turn births worship, it will leave us empty. But why? Because we were made to live lives pointing to God.

When you rise above yourself and your purpose in life is no longer about you, but God, you will be able to stare midnight in the face and say, "Bring it on. You may be big, but my God is bigger."

Fighting Against Riptide

Have you ever been to the beach and been pulled out into the ocean by a riptide? I have never been pulled out deep, but I have had my pants pulled down when I was a child. One moment I was boogie boarding, and the next I was in my birthday suit in front of everyone.

Nearly forty-six people a year die from riptides alone.[ii] See, what makes a riptide so dangerous is the constant pull it has back towards the deep.

From what I have rationed in my twenty-one years of life, there are **three significant** riptides that pull us out from where God wants us to be and into the deep waters of faithlessness.

The riptide of natural human *thought*. Growing up, I heard the phrase, "God gave you a mind, son, so use it." But sometimes our thoughts do not line up with God's. Human reason in and of itself is not a bad thing. In fact, human reason keeps us out of a lot of trouble. Just don't forget, at times, human reason and God's plans differ.

Natural human *tendency* can also be a good thing. It is a natural human tendency to run from persecution. If you don't believe me, just allow a murderer to walk through your front door with a gun. The first thing you will do is run—either to a weapon or from one. It is a natural reaction—fight or flight. It is also a natural human tendency to be attracted to what is *conceived* by you to be best.

If a kid walks into a room and has the choice between eating a piece of lettuce or a piece of candy, the child will most likely choose the candy, depending on the kid, because it is our natural human tendency to move towards what we deem is best and away from anything else.

The *culture* also implores many things of us—namely, to buy into its system of measuring success. I will talk later about this, but culture has a massive pull in our lives. The way we choose right and wrong, the music we listen to, and the relationships that we pursue are all affected by culture. A hot topic of discussion today is, "Does culture shape morality?" I think it does, but God doesn't back away from that. Afterall, God made culture.

Now you **may be thinking,** *Drake, why tell us about these things? Do they have a point?*

Yes, they do, and here it is: It is not reasonable to have joy in the midst of adversity. It is unusual to be found in a condition where you can worship God during the worst moments of life. It is even more rare to find purpose in the midst of tragedy. To get there, you will have to fight against these three riptides that all have a continual pull on your life. But before you can fight against them, you must **recognize** what they are. They must be called out like that bully in high school. These riptides are similar to cancer; until you identify them, they are impossible to oppose. 1) The riptide of natural human thought. 2) Natural human tendency. 3) The culture.

Now that we have identified these three bullies, let's get to work!

My Story: II

A few minutes after arriving at UMMC, an uneasy feeling formed in the pit of my stomach that clawed at the core of my being. Fear. **Fear's antidote is faith and the soundtrack of faith is worship.**[iii] When pushed to his visceral limit, a man will do almost anything to ensure survival—especially for those whom he loves. So, you could imagine my sense of helplessness as Catherine's destiny lay beyond my control.

The doctor stepped foot into Catherine's room and began to speak, "I have been looking at your test results from the MRI and blood work. I have a few questions I would like to ask: First, did you have any complications at birth?"

Catherine, conscious enough to respond, shook her head to indicate she hadn't.

"Well then, would you possibly be a twin?"

"Yes," Catherine uttered.

"Excellent. You are the second born, no?"

"Uh, huh. How did you know?"

"Okay, Catherine. I have some good news," the doctors said. "I don't think those clots seen on the scan are brain bleeds at all. I think they are cysts. Sometimes, babies with complications at birth or who are twins will develop these spinal fluid cysts. In your case, I think you've had them since birth.

"What happens is spinal fluid builds up and leaks into the brain. Overtime, this hardens, and the brain grows around it. This is exactly what I think we are seeing here with you."

"So, what are you saying? Am I going to be okay? I'm not going to die?"

"No Miss. Moultrie. You'll be just fine. I am going to schedule you in for a follow up appointment within the next six months to track any growth in these cysts. You're free to go after we run a few more tests. Also, you might want to call your parents and let them know you're okay. I am sure they are worried sick."

A few minutes passed by until the information drifted down to my room. I wanted to run around and jump for joy, but my intravenous bag said otherwise. I was still dealing with a grade three concussion and a sprained T-Spine. The Phenergan was nice, but it was quickly tapering down.

The day ended with the doctors releasing both Catherine and I to go home. At one point in the not too distant past, our departure from UMMC seemed only to be imaginary, but here we were, walking out hand in hand.

That being said, I thought the car wreck was the end of bad things to come. Little did I know, it was just the beginning.

MW

CHAPTER THREE

THE KEY TO MIDNIGHT

When I was in high school, I dreamed of becoming a professional golfer. I did not only dream this way; I made a life of it.

Each day after school, I would listen to sermons by Judah Smith, or Francis Chan, or Louie Giglio, or really just whoever, while I practiced day after day, year after year. Eventually, I got pretty good.

During my tenth-grade year, I was playing in the district tournament at Quail Hollow. (No, not the real Quail Hollow in North Carolina—this was the generic Mississippi Quail Hollow. Also, I would like to go on record here and admit that while I was playing, a sprinkler came on and shot me right in the butt. *Yes, it gave me a water enema.* "*What's so bad about that?*" you ask? Well, this was no normal sprinkler. Oh no. It lifted me off the ground. I finished the rest of my round soaking wet and butthurt. Literally!)

I was playing against golfers who were much better than I, but after eighteen holes, I found myself tied for the lead. The round consisted of a few birdies and one driver off the deck shot that landed six foot from the hole for eagle. To this day, that is my most memorable shot.

A few holes before, on sixteen, I made a ten-foot-long par putt that gave me the lead, but soon lost it on seventeen when I missed the green with my approach.

As I stood on the eighteenth green, tied for the lead, in the last group of the day, I had just one more job: make about a six-foot par putt to win. I got up to the putt, but my hands wouldn't quit shaking. Not to mention, my entire team was on the hillside beside the green cheering me on.

Before I walked up to the putt, my dad came up beside me to give one last motivational speech, "Son, these moments don't come around every day. Make the most of your opportunity." *Thanks dad, that really calms my nerves—not.*

I walked back up to the putt after backing off to catch my breath, prayed, and then sent the little white ball rolling towards the hole.

Looking back, I often reflect on all the practice that went into that one moment. The hours of preparation spent on the driving range. The previous seventeen holes all boiled down to one putt. All the hard work and the foundation that had been laid was to prepare me for that one moment—to be able to step up to the putt with the confidence that it was going in. And this is what chapter three is all about.

All the groundwork has been laid for these next few moments. This chapter has the opportunity to change the rest of your life absolutely. (I was using Grammarly to edit the second and third rounds of manuscript sanctification—that's what I call it anyways—and it told me to change the last sentence by adding *absolutely* towards the end. I thought it sounded cool, so I stuck with it. Hope you like.)

Now, I know what many of you are asking, "So, did you make the putt?" You'll have to wait and find out. ☺

The two main questions that we ask when midnights begin are the *why* question and the *how* question. *Why am I going through this?* and *How do I get through it?* In many cases, we never know the *why* behind God allowing us to go through midnights. I do have a few ideas...

- It could be to reach other people in their midnight, as was the case for Paul and Silas.
- It could be to strengthen our endurance so that our faith will grow as James suggests.
- It could be to strengthen our walk with Christ.
- It could be to teach us a lesson we would not learn any other way.

There are many different possibilities as to why we go through midnights. However, when the clock strikes twelve, we often cannot see the *why*. **The fingerprints of God are often invisible until you look at them through the rearview mirror.**[i] It is not until years later we can look back on things and understand. Sometimes we never get that understanding or clarity, do we?

There is also a plethora of different ways to answer the *how* question. People cope with their midnights differently. Some people are suppressors. They suppress all their emotions and feelings until it all boils over, and they explode. Some people are drinkers. They find their peace at the bottom of a bottle, numbing all the pain. Some are over-reactors. Some are under-reactors. Some are overeaters. Some are over thinkers. Some try to find someone to hold. And others want to be held.

Still, others try to find someone to fight. Some find someone to shift the blame on. Some try to find something to occupy their time. And some try to fill their minds, keeping it off the fact that they're struggling. Yet, none of these approaches are what Paul and Silas decided to do in their midnight. After they were beaten and thrown into jail, they chose to worship.

Honestly, I cannot tell you why you have gone through everything you have, nor would I pretend to know every step your shoes have walked. But I do know this; worship is more than just our purpose in life or a service-plaguing euphoria; it is our anchor.

MY STORY: III

The following weeks after the concussion, I had trouble remembering anything at all. I would forget things that I didn't even know were possible. Like once, I walked out of my dorm room headed to class with no shorts or shirt on. (You're probably thinking, *"What's wrong with that bro? I do that all the time!"* If you saw what I looked like without a shirt on, you would know exactly the problem with that scenario.)

One time I went to New Orleans when I meant to go to Jackson, Mississippi; all because I forgot where I was going. Isn't that crazy? My geometry teacher used to joke saying, "You can solve the equation like that if you want, but that's like driving to Jackson through Gulfport." Well Mr. Bobby Lee, I can honestly say I've driven to Jackson through New Orleans—much worse. Also, I cannot tell you how many times in three months I went to Chick-fil-A instead of Walmart. Not that a Chick-fil-A sandwich is a problem, but it's not Walmart and doesn't sell toilet paper.

On the surface, it seems to be more of an inconvenience than a problem, but the problem came when I had to take finals to graduate from Mississippi College. Studying was like pouring water into a cup with a hole in the bottom. Everything that I studied, I soon forgot. I spent thirty hours studying for one test, but no matter how hard I studied, I couldn't retain the information. The stress of knowing that I had fifteen-thousand dollars invested in one semester of school was enough to drive anyone crazy. But that was just the beginning.

At the same time, Catherine began to get migraine headaches every day. Due to her two cysts discovered in the wreck, she went to a new neurologist what seemed like every week. On the inside, Catherine was having a nervous breakdown. I cannot go into much detail about Catherine's health. Honestly, we still do not know much about it. But for about three months, she was completely out of commission.

At the same time, I began to notice an unusual growth on my left cheek. I ignored it for as long as I could, thinking it would go away. But after a few months of not getting any better, I decided to go to the doctor to get it looked at. The doctor I was recommended to told me I needed a CAT scan to make sure that I didn't have cancer.

Cancer? I thought as the doctor was writing my prescription. *I am only twenty-one years old. What are you using a word like that for?* However, life comes fast; we do nothing to earn it, and just as it was given, it can be taken.

That was the first time I heard *cancer* directed towards me. The likelihood of having it was low, but the thought of *what if* dominated my mind. On December 2nd, I went in for my first scan. I can remember sitting down getting all the shots and thinking to myself, *"Wow, this is actually the first time in a long time I have been able to sit down."* After eight attempts to start an IV, (seriously, I counted the pinpricks in my arm afterward) the nurse finally got a vein. That was the beginning of many different CAT scans.

December 8th came and went, but I was not ready for what was headed my way. Due to how personal the information is, I cannot explain everything that happened. Trust me; you really don't care to know. But life came at me, and I was at an all-time low—completely overwhelmed. I was just trying to endure; just trying to get through life. I wasn't depressed, nor would I say I had severe anxiety over the situation. To be honest, I can't describe how I felt, but there I was—waiting. Waiting on my grades to come back to see if I passed the classes. Waiting for my test results to see what this growth was on the side of my face. Waiting on Catherine's doctor's report to find out if she needed brain surgery.

I was trying to be the leader our youth group needed. Trying to be the leader my family needed. Trying to be the boyfriend Catherine needed. Not to mention, I was trying to hold myself together all the while. I felt like I was going insane. Stress rose on every side of me, so I decided to do what I usually do when I am stressed: clean stuff.

I had just listened to a sermon where the pastor talked about his anxiety, and how in his stress, a song arose that helped him endure through it. So, I already had that thought in the back of my mind. As I went to clean out my vehicle, I turned the radio on, when suddenly *Lord I Need You* by Matt Maher came on. It goes like this:

> "Lord, I need you,
> Oh I need you.
> Every hour I need you,
> You're my one defense
> My righteousness,
> Oh God, how I need you."

I sang it, replayed it, then sang it again. That song was stuck in my head throughout that month. I held on to it like a drowning man holds on to a plank of wood in a shipwreck. I can't explain it, but I just kept singing that song—like, all the time.

December came and went. I eventually got my test results back. I am just telling my story, so please give me grace on this, but the worship continued throughout January. If you're wondering what happened in my narrative: I passed my classes; Catherine is headed right now to the Mayo Clinic in Jacksonville, Florida; my memory is better but still not the same as it was; and doctors still don't know what's wrong with my face. In fact, as I type, my left ear is ringing from the swelling in my jaw. And that's okay! Because through it all, anchored in me, was and is, the key to midnight.

Please understand this; worship will not cause your problems to go away. If you think that and you begin to worship, but your problems come back, you will abandon your faith, your worship, and possibly your God. Desmond Doss, after winning his Congressional Medal of Honor, got tuberculosis, lost a lung and five ribs, and, at the age of seventy, lost his wife.

No. Worship does not cause your problems to magically disappear, although sometimes God will take them away. But what worship does is place in us the power and ability to withstand whatever the enemy throws at us and whatever midnights come our way. I do not know the *why* behind your midnight, but I do know that worship is the *how*.

Remember that Mockingbird that was singing outside my room? I learned another important lesson from that bird; PRAISES IN THE NIGHT BRING FREEDOM FOR THE MORNING.

Praises in the night bring freedom for the morning

SHELTER FROM THE STORM

As I'm typing this, I am on a youth trip in Panama City (This was one of the first things I typed in *Midnight Worship*. Me and Catherine haven't even met yet just in case you're wondering how I'm driving to the Mayo Clinic and on a youth trip in Panama City at the same time.). I came with my old youth pastor to help lead a small group. We planned all kinds of different games to entertain the kids between the worship services, but Hurricane Alberto decided it had different plans.

The wind picked up at about eight o'clock this morning, and for the last five hours it has come a downpour. The storm has become so bad that water tornados have begun to form. (I don't even know what a water tornado is. I'm about to ask somebody. It sounds pretty devastating though.)

We took shelter in the auditorium this morning.

While Hurricane Alberto made its landfall, the band got on stage and began to play. In the middle of that storm, we sat in the auditorium, and a hundred and fifty kids worshiped God—IN THE MIDDLE OF A HURRICANE. How crazy is that? I could not help but get lost in the worship. Here I am, praying to God for inspiration for this book and, in the middle of a hurricane, a band gets up and we all sing praises to God. Then it hits me; *I need to write this in the book.* A lightbulb went off, and I think Jesus is trying to tell us today—tell you today—worship will not only get us through the storm, **BUT WORSHIP IS OUR SHELTER FROM IT**.

> But worship is our shelter from it.

It holds us together. It binds us. It makes us one. It holds us in the storm. It supports us. It fills us with his Spirit.

In the middle of the storm that we face, when we worship God, we find peace—we find rest. And that is where we find safety. Do you need peace in your storm?

Worship God!

Peace is not found at the bottom of a Bud Light can, for that is only temporary. Peace is not found in sex, pills, eating, or any other way we try to cope with the fact that we are hurting. True peace is found in worship. No matter the storm, prison, midnight, hard time, valley, or battle you are going through, if you need shelter, sing out to God.

This is the song that the band is playing now:

> *"Great are You, Lord*
> *It's Your breath in our lungs*
> *So we pour out our praise*
> *We pour out our praise*
> *It's Your breath in our lungs*
> *So we pour out our praise to You only."*

Literally, as this storm blows through, and as the winds gush, and as the waves crash, one hundred and fifty kids are singing those lyrics at the top of their lungs. Wow—**thank you, God, for our safety, your presence, and the inspiration that you have given me. Please bless the person reading this to know that in the middle of their hurricane, when they worship you, they will find the shelter they need. Please help them in their understanding that worship is the key to midnight. Amen.**

I made the putt by the way. #ice

MW

INTERLUDE

ROOMS OF UNANSWERED PRAYERS

It is not my primary intention through these next few chapters to justify why God does not answer all prayers; however, that will certainly be a topic of discussion. My ultimate goal is to discuss six difficult areas of loss—**vulnerability, death, failed relationships, broken dreams, mental ill-health, and a fractured past**—in a way that helps you understand the bigger picture and see the goodness of God through the darkness of the night.

Many prayers go unanswered. I don't need to tell you that, just look around you. I believe many more prayers are answered than vice versa, and I believe in the power of prayer. But an unanswered prayer can create a numbness that causes hostility towards God. Your prayer life, for instance, can become the summation of, "never get my hopes up, so I'll never be let down."

Maybe you find yourself having a conversation like Timothy and Paul:

Timothy- "My stomach is hurting"

Paul- "Was it something you ate buddy?"

Timothy- "I don't think. You know I have stomach problems. Can you not help me? Maybe take this pain away?"

Paul- "Am I God that I can heal your stomach?"

Timothy walked to the other side of the room, poured a glass of water, and said:

Timothy- "Paul, I don't understand you. You heal people every day of all sorts of diseases, but you can't heal my stomach?"

Smiling, Paul rubbed Timothy's shoulders, and replied, "I've never healed anyone buddy. God did."

This little conversation between Paul and Timothy is not in the Bible, but I wonder if it ever happened? We know that Paul healed many people (see Acts 14:8, Acts 19:12). We also know that Timothy had a stomach ailment (See 1 Timothy 5:23). Out of all the miracles Paul did, why didn't he heal Timothy? Was he unthoughtful? Unfaithful? No. I don't think that's it.

See, Paul had many prayer requests go unanswered also. Like when Paul prayed for God to take away his *thorn in the flesh*. God answered him by saying, "My strength works best in your weakness" (2 Corinthians 12:9, NLT). So God healed many people through Paul, but when it came to him, there was no healing.

To which I think, *"What? Are you kidding me? That makes no sense. Why didn't healing happen? Why didn't God answer his prayer? Why didn't he come through?"*

Truth be told, we all think things like this when we pray but hear no response, don't we?

God's idea may not be to take us out of the midnight; it may be to guide us through it, and if not through it, then to him. Let me say that again for emphasis: God's idea may not be to take us out of the midnight. Rather, it may be to carry us through it, and if not through it, then to him.

MW

CHAPTER FOUR

ROOM OF DEATH

As we begin this chapter, I want to share with you a story from the perspective of an amazing woman who we call Jack.

JACK'S STORY: FROM WEEPING TO WORSHIP

Drake asked me to tell my story, so no promises, but I will do my best.

I have experienced three major travesties in the seventy-eight years spent on planet Earth. The first being the loss of my two boys during their early twenties. The second was the diagnosis of Multiple Sclerosis, and the third was the divorce and death of my husband. Before we go any further, I want to share with you my favorite hymn;

> *Amazing grace! How sweet the sound?*
> *That saved a wretch; like me!*
> *I once was lost, but now am found,*
> *Was blind, but now I see.*

"Unanswered Prayer.
Or so I Thought"

Having three fine boys, I decided to have one last child and dedicate him or her to the LORD. I was blessed to have my fourth son, Tyson.

After having the child, I spent the next week in prayer asking the LORD to use Tyson's life for his kingdom.

Tyson was saved when he was about twelve and was baptized, but he never seemed to be turned to preach or go into ministry in any way. He seemed more involved with sports. After graduation, he soon married and went to work at Georgia Pacific. Being human, I grew impatient and puzzled that God had not answered my prayer. However, I kept that prayer of dedication in my heart and in the back of my mind.

Tyson had a son whom, from the beginning, I could tell was different. I would notice every time I would go to clean his room, his Bible would move from his bed, to the den, to his shelf, to his dresser. So, one day, I asked him about it. He told me he read it every night before he went to sleep. I watched him grow up from that little boy into the man he is today, and all of a sudden, one day, it hit me. God answered my prayer from all those years ago, not in Tyson, but through him. I became convicted of my impatience and thanked God for his remembrance of my prayers those many years ago.

I say that as a metanarrative of my life's story. God has not always answered my prayers as I thought he should. My life has not gone as planned—BUT—I can stand before you today as a testament to God's faithfulness through the storm. By the Grace of God, I can say, through all the midnights in my life, God is greater.

"My Boys"

The day death crept into my reality was a Saturday in May. As I pulled into my house, cars lined the driveway and filled the front yard. I don't know how, but I instantly knew one of my children had been killed. As I got out, my brain started to work so fast. *Was there one of my boys that I loved more? Could I lose any of them?* I began to back up and cuff my hands over my ears. I didn't want to know which one of my sons I would never hold again. People came out to the driveway and began putting their arms around me, hugging me, but I didn't want any part of it. I continued with my ears cuffed until someone leaned over and said, "It's Tony."

Tony was my oldest, and instantly, my heart was ingulfed with grief. He was twenty-six years old, but it felt like only yesterday I was taking him home from the hospital. I cannot remember much else from that day; I was in a daze. I cannot recall many details of the funeral, and to be honest, I don't want to.

However, I handled his death pretty well. I stayed strong because I knew I had three other boys to raise. I had to be the emotional rock for them. So I was.

A few years went by until, one night, the phone rang in the wee hours of the morning with the news only present in my worst nightmares. "Janice," the voice on the other end of the line said, "We have some...well see, there is no easy way to say this, but we have some bad news. Tim has just gotten in a wreck and is being airlifted to Tupelo's hospital." His father and I immediately jumped in the car.

Bill, my husband, and I kept quiet. I prayed the entire ride, "God, please just let him be alive; even if he has to be bedridden, I will spend the rest of my life at his bedside. Just please, God, let him live."

As we turned onto Natchez Trace Parkway in Jackson, Mississippi, my heart literally turned inside my chest. I was overtaken by deep emotion. I hollered to my husband, "He is dead. I know it. What time is it?" It was 7:09 a.m.

We didn't speak another word. I couldn't talk. I was numb. I was beside myself. I cannot explain it, but glimmering within me was an inkling of hope. Nobody asks to be in an emergency room. We certainly didn't. Death doesn't call ahead.

When we arrived at the hospital, it was too late; Tim was dead. *Hurting with hope still hurts.*[i]

The first thought that entered was, *"I'm surely going to die; there is no way my heart can take this."*

Once again, I cannot remember the funeral or anything in the following weeks. But I later found out that Tim died at 7:09 a.m.—the exact time I told my husband.

After the funeral, all I did was cry. I handled the death of Tony well, but this one messed me up. Not because I loved Tim any more than Tony, but the compound interest of losing two children by the age of fifty broke me. I can remember sitting up at night as the hot tears rolled down my cheeks. I know it sounds crazy, but all I wanted to do was touch their skin one last time. I wanted to dig them up out of the ground. It was my fault; they were my responsibility. I was their mother, and the last place I left them was in the dirt. I felt like a failure. I was only forty-nine, and I had lost two sons—how could I go on?

I remember the first time I laughed after the death of Tim. I felt guilty; my two sons are dead, and here I am smiling. It wasn't right. Perhaps grief discuses itself as humility.

When a woman's husband dies, she is called a widow. If it's the husband who survives, he is called a widower. Children who lose their parents are called orphans. But what do you call a mom or dad who loses a child? There is no title for that. I suppose because there are no words to describe such a thing.[i] However, if there is one word to describe how I felt, it was numb. Numb to everything and angry with God. Upset that he would allow this to happen. *How could a God that loved me take away something I cared so much for?*

- I fell deep into depression.
- I couldn't stop crying.
- I couldn't go to work.
- I couldn't find joy.
- I couldn't find God, nor did I want to.

I wanted an answer. I wanted God to answer me; "Why God, why did you allow this to happen?" My grief did not end. It kept on. It was the hardest time in my life—the time when I should have turned to God, but I turned away. How was I supposed to pray? How was I supposed to thank him? "Thank you, God, for making my life hell?" No. So I didn't pray nor did I draw near to God in the lowest moments.

I think it is funny this book is titled *Midnight Worship*. I guess you could say my midnight lasted a while—nine years to be exact. I stayed in that hole of depression, anger, anxiety, grief, and misery for nine years.

"God, why did you let this happen?" "Why did you take away my sons—my crowns of inheritance?" "Can I have them back?" For nine years, I prayed prayers like this.

I am not just saying this because of the title of the book, but literally, AT ABOUT MIDNIGHT, while praying a prayer similar to this one, I realized that God did not cause my sons to be killed. It was not his fault they died: it was theirs.

It did not happen overnight, but through the course of the next year I learned to thank God for the years that he had given me with my boys. I learned to flip the script in the way I viewed their lives. Eventually, I got back what had been taken from me so long ago: thankfulness. I know this does not sound like much, but it took me nine years to get to this point. Even though it was a small one, I felt like it was a victory.

If there is one thing that I can go on record saying in this book, it is, *"Even when you can't see the morning; even when you don't know why; even when you DON'T WANT TO; Thank God."*

"My Marriage and His Death"

After only courting my husband for two months, we married in late 1957. Our marriage was unique. My husband passed away in 2007 of a heart attack. We divorced a few years before his death in 2003. I will not disrespect my late husband by speaking ill of him. Just know, I could fill this entire book with stories of what we went through as a family.

Though my marriage, our divorce, and his death were huge parts of my life, I will not write more on the subject due to the sensitivity and vulnerability of the situation, and also out of respect for my children and grandchildren who will read this book.

"Multiple Sclerosis"

Years before my divorce, pains began to develop in my upper right hip. For twenty-six years, every few months my body would show signs of an illness. I would experience dizziness, tingling in my legs, debilitating fatigue, nausea, and all sorts of other symptoms too numerous to count.

I went from doctor to doctor to find out what was wrong, but every doctor I saw told me the symptoms were in my head. That I was okay. After hearing the same thing from several doctors, I soon began to accept the fact that no one could help me. I knew my symptoms were real because they were real to me!

Eventually, I quit going and learned to deal with the symptoms. They only flared up every six months to a year and lasted about two weeks. I could manage life that way.

The day M.S. became debilitating, I was fifty-seven and working at Lawrence County Hospital as a nurse. I got up to get dressed but couldn't get out of bed.

Rachel Broom, one of my best friends at the time, came and took me to the University Medical Center in Jackson. By this time, the MRI machine had come onto the market, so they ran every kind of test you can think of. The doctor came in, and with almost a saddened spirit, looked me in the eyes and told me words I will never forget, "Mrs. Janice, I am sorry to say this, but you have Multiple Sclerosis."

To his astonishment, I was happy. I broke into tears of joy. I finally knew what was wrong with me. After twenty-six years of doctors telling me it was all in my head, for the first time, I had a real diagnosis. I had something to tell other people. If any of you have been in that place of having an un-diagnosable illness, you can feel my relief when my sickness was named.

Multiple Sclerosis is a disease that attacks the central nervous system, the brain, the optic nerves, and the spinal cord. Its symptoms vary: numbness of a limb, blurred vision, sensations of electric shock in the body. The root of the problem is brain damage, which causes your nerve endings to dissipate. (Turns out the other doctors were right all along, it really was all in my head; my brain was dying.)

I was hospitalized five times throughout the first year. Once, I was intubated and rushed to UMMC. The pains in my right hip and leg were unbearable. I couldn't walk. I was bed-bound. The pain monopolized my life.

I am seventy-eight years young now. I have had eight surgeries to help fight the pain that M.S. causes. I have recently gotten a spine stimulator put into my back to help ease the pain, and it has given me more relief than ever, though I still hurt constantly. Even now, as I write, I am in bed because of the pain in my right hip. Though the pain hasn't ceased, and I know tomorrow will bring troubles, I serve a God who is Lord. Even Lord over Multiple Sclerosis.

"My Conclusion: A Doxology to a Glorious God"

Through it all, I have left God at times—but he has never left me. I will praise him for holding on to me. I thank him for the gift of repentance that he has so graciously accepted. My heart has been comforted by

Those midnight hours have turned from weeping to worship.

the fact that my prayer from so long ago was answered, and I am alive to see it materialize.

We have no power apart from God; our next breath is dependent upon him. It took me going through midnight to understand that, but I am thankful for the lesson. I still have M.S., but I can walk. My two sons are dead, but I will see them again. My husband may have passed, but I have remarried, and in my later days, I am happy.

Believe me when I say, I have had my share of dark sleepless nights filled with many tears. BUT thanks be to God—*Those midnight hours have turned from weeping to worship.*

What is Death?

Before we discuss specific factions that stem from death, we must set the foundation of what death is—the implications of it.

To define death, *it is the physical body's ending that gives way to the spiritual body's eternal affair.* Another way to think about it is, *death is a doorway, not a stagnant domain.*

Conceptually, we know that death is inevitable. We know that Heaven is better. But when death comes, we lose our depiction of reality.

It's logical that humans do this. Due to the pain of losing a loved one, it very well should be that we lose our touch with reality. But what is reality? The reality of death is that it brings way to life. Joseph Solomon wrote this concerning his relationship with God: "Through sickness and in health, through faith and through questions, until death brings us closer, you are mine, and I am yours."[ii]

Death causes a lack of knowledge of objectivity. We see only a fraction of the whole picture. You see this in a teenager who is in love. Everyone tells her that she should break up with LJ because he is no good for her, but she loves him. He accepts her for who she is. And acceptance, like love, is a powerful force. So her reality is distorted by love and acceptance.

You can also see this in sports. A ref makes a logical call on the field, but because one likes the team the call went against, (s)he screams, "Ref, you're blind! Get some glasses!" Though it was a logical call, their vision is biased. Well, the same is true when it comes to Christians facing death. We know the grave gives way to life, but we lose our depiction of this truth during the aftermath of heartbreak so unbearable it can't be expressed with words. We lose sight of our irreducible minimum.

THE IRREDUCIBLE MINIMUM

My friends and I have always been close, but we have had our fair share of arguments as well. I can remember the angriest I've ever been with my best friend, Smoot.

I had just gotten a new deer stand in late December, but before I could use it, I had to take my final exams. I left the stand at the hunting camp for the time being and drove up to Mississippi College.

Well, Smoot decided to take my stand out for a spin. After all, isn't that what best friends do?

When I finished with school, I drove over to the hunting camp, but couldn't find my stand anywhere. It was about dark, so I decided to pick up Smoot and see if he had seen anything.

As he walked in the parking lot, I noticed he was moving a bit odd. But as soon as he got in the truck, I smelt it.

"Smoot, what is that smell, man? Did you crap yourself?"

"How did you know?" he responded.

"Because I could smell you from the tailgate. You stink…Wait, is that what I think it is? Is that my stand?"

"Don't be mad bra. I couldn't find mine, so I just borrowed yours."

I jumped out of the driver's seat and looked at my stand…Crap all over it.

"You know how it is," Smoot explained. "I was like twenty-five feet up a tree, and it hit me." (It takes about three minutes to quickly climb down a tree and five minutes to do it safely.)

"I didn't have any time to spare. I had to GO. I tried leaning off the edge, but I guess some fell on the bottom part of the climbing stand without me knowing."

I walked over to look at Smoot's back—poop smeared everywhere. The smell was potent.

"Take your clothes off, lay them in the bed of the truck, and let's go."

No joke, I went to Bass Pro the next week and bought a brand-new stand.

"You can keep the poop stand, Smoot."

In that moment, twenty-five feet in the air, Smoot discovered his irreducible minimum. It wasn't seeing deer, safety, or the coldness. His irreducible minimum was…well, you know…

See, what death tends to do is reverse our irreducible minimum. If you're still a little confused by what irreducible minimum means, simply put, it is the concern that rises to the top of our priority list. For example, if we couldn't breathe, our irreducible minimum would be oxygen.

And that's what it feels like when someone passes, isn't it? That we can't breathe. That our heart has been ripped out. The reason death does this is because there is no more fighting. Until death comes, people often go from one doctor to another, fighting, but now that they're gone, there is no going back; there is no more trying; there is no last word. Even worse, sometimes we are given no fighting time. Instead, we are left to pick up the pieces of a sudden death. Thoughts begin to drop like bombs:

If I could have only told them how I felt.
Cooked them one last meal.
Kissed them one last time.
Danced with them one last song.

When Catherine arrived at the hospital, everyone there thought she was going to die—including me. After all, that's what I was told. I remember thinking in that moment; *It's all my fault; Catherine is going to die, and it is all my fault.* I remember asking God to save her, and honestly, I didn't pray that prayer for her, but for me. The guilt that I felt because I was the reason she was dying. I didn't want to live with that; I didn't know if I could.

Are any of you there now? Someone close to you died, and you feel the blame. You feel the responsibility—like you caused the death, or could have done something to stop it, but you didn't, and now they're gone? That misery is unthwarted.

Even if you know it wasn't your fault, you may still feel guilt for letting it happen. Guilt for not being strong enough, not being able to stop it, not having the right information, not making the right decisions. **God does not want you to feel that shame, that regret, that remorse, that guilt.**

You may ask, "Drake, how can you even say that? How can you possibly know? You don't know my situation. You don't know what I did or didn't do. If you did, you would take back the previous statement." Well, listen to what Scripture says, "What is the price of two sparrows—one copper coin? But not a single sparrow can fall to the ground without your Father knowing it." (Matt. 10:29, NIV)

In other words, God is not surprised.

In the history of forever, God has never said to someone in Heaven, "Hmm, surprised to see you here. I didn't think you were coming until your late seventies. How did you even get here?"

Maybe *you are* the reason that someone is gone, and now you're feeling the weight on your shoulders for their death. I don't want to gloss over that. You drove drunk; you didn't secure the foundation; you caused the secondhand smoke. If that's you, I encourage you to skip to chapter twelve and then come back and finish. Just know, there is life beyond this one. You have been forgiven. Now forgive yourself.

On the same note, *is it possible for good to stem from death?*

Look at Acts 8.

Stephen, who is the first Christian martyr, was stoned to death. But during the stoning, Stephen prayed, "Lord Jesus, receive my spirit." He fell to his knees, shouting, "Lord, don't charge them with this sin!" *And then he died.* (See Acts 7:59-60)

Then, in verse one of the following chapter, Scripture says, speaking of Stephen's death, "A great wave of persecution began that day, sweeping over the church in Jerusalem; and all the believers except the apostles, were scattered through the regions of Judea and Samaria. (Some devout men came and buried Stephen with great mourning.) But Saul was going everywhere to destroy the church. He went from house to house, dragging out both men and women to throw them into prison." (Acts 8:1-3, NLT)

After reading those verses, logically I thought, "So what? Persecution broke out, and people were thrown into prison. What's the big idea?" But keep reading!

"But the believers who were scattered preached the Good News about Jesus wherever they went." (Acts 8:4, NLT)

Because of persecution, the Gospel spread through Judea and Samaria while the Apostles held it down in Jerusalem. More evangelism came through Stephen's death than fifty years of his living. Little did Saul know at the time, he would be a contributor to completing the Great Commission and taking the Good News to the ends of the World. If Saul can turn his story from *per-*

secutor to *pastor* and the story of Stephen can go from *mourning* to *ministry,* you can have a comeback story as well. Don't quit! Keep pursuing God!

Silent Night

I woke up this morning to the door swinging open and Dad yelling for my mother to get up: "Christy, wake up! Come outside! Somebody needs your help!" I knew something was wrong, so I immediately jumped to my feet and followed him outside. (I was sleeping on the couch btw. #lifeofacollegestudent)

Mom is a nurse and I heard sirens in the distance, so I knew something had to be severely wrong. I turned the corner of my garage, and then...I saw her. A young woman I didn't even know, with two children standing over her. There she lay: not breathing; outside in the grass; the two children surrounding her; and from what I could tell—dead. Another ambulance soon arrived, and her two children sat watching as the EMTs tried their best to save their mother.

As I type this, I don't know what's going to happen. I have been praying for her constantly for the last twenty minutes—a simple prayer really; "God, please breathe life back into her as only you can do." I don't know if my prayer will be answered, but can you imagine the heartache the family is going through right now. Literally, walking through the valley of the shadow of death, minds spinning a hundred miles an hour, and in the coming months, much more pain to walk through. Some of you have been there.

I was thinking to myself as I came to the end of this chapter, *"Hmm, maybe I can give them this book when it gets published. Perhaps it will help."* Truth is, no amount of reading will satisfy; no wise word will counsel. It is not in the heat of the moment that healing will come, but only minutes before or years after. That being said, I want to ask the question, "What happens in those years of silence, and is there any way to bring comfort into that quiet place?"

I think that there is, but only to a certain extent.

David knew all too well what the silence felt like. Many nights found David lying on his pillow sobbing uncontrollably. In the midst of it all, he cried out to God, "My God, my God, why have you abandoned me? Why are you so far away when I groan for help? Every day I call to you, my God, but you do not answer. Every night I lift my voice, but I find no relief." (Psalm 22:1-2, NLT)

David had lost a son, cried himself to sleep, hadn't heard from God, and in the next chapter, wrote the most famous passage in Scripture: Psalm 23.

Job too, knew the long nights of silence. He spent thirty-eight chapters crying out to God, hoping for an answer. He had lost his ten children, his friends, his possessions, his reputation, his health; but what did Job get in response after pleading with God to be heard? Nothing! He got NOTHING.

I have been there before—crying out to God, asking him to speak, only to get silence.

Lysa TerKeurst, after finding out her husband was cheating days before being hospitalized due to the excruciating pain of her colon ripping, wrote:

"As the panic began to give way to desperation, I cried out for God to help me. 'Take the pain away! Please, dear God, take this pain away!' But he didn't. Not that moment. Not the next. Not even the next day. His silence stunned me. How could God do that? How could he say I'm his daughter whom he deeply loves but let me lie there in excruciating pain? I have children. And if I could take away their pain, without a doubt I would. God could do that. But he was choosing not to.

I kept picturing him standing beside my bed seeing my anguish, watching my body writhing in pain, hearing my cries but making the choice to do nothing. And I couldn't reconcile that. It's the same thing that happens when I hear of a baby being stillborn. Or a young mother dying of cancer. Or a teenager committing suicide. Or someone suffering in a refugee camp. Or people starving in a third-world country. Where are you, God? I mean, even humans with the slightest bit of compassion are compelled to do something to help another person in deep distress and pain.

A few years ago, my husband and I witnessed a terrible car accident. Without even thinking, our instincts were immediately to help. We didn't even know these people. We never even found out their names. But we couldn't just drive by and do nothing. I don't say this to shine some sort of halo over our heads. I'm just saying, as imperfect as we are, we were compelled to do something. So, how can a perfect God seemingly stay silent at times?"[iii]

Have any of you been there? In the silence? Asking God why? This is where Job found himself, but eventually, God broke the muteness and responded:

"Where were you when I laid the earth's foundation?
Tell me, if you understand.
Who marked off its dimensions? Surely you know!
Who stretched a measuring line across it?
Who shut up the sea behind doors
when it burst forth from the womb?"
(Job 38:4-6, 8, NIV)

Sometimes God won't give you a reason; he will give you a revelation.[iv] After thirty-eight chapters of nothingness, God finally responded, but in his four-chapter soliloquy, Job never had his questions answered. God never told him why he took his children or made a mess of his life. God just started asking questions. **God never gave Job the answer he wanted, but he gave the answer he needed.** The same is true of you.

You may be in the silent years during the aftermath of a plethora of questions rationed by you, all with the underlining foundation, "Why, God?" Your family has been taken; your wife has been taken; it feels like life has slipped through your fingers; it feels like life is pointless.

I can't promise you will get the answer you want, and I can't guarantee God will respond as soon as you'd hope. But I can assure you that God will give you what you need. Job responds after walking through devastation by saying, "Even though he slay me, yet I will trust in him." (Job 13:15, KJV)

I encourage you to declare the same, "Though I do not hear, yet I will trust in you."

DOES GOD EVEN CARE?

After reading all this, you may think, "Drake, that's all well and good, but that's not really what I need to know right now. What I need to know is, does God see me, does he care, and can he do something?"

I want to show you a promise from God. It reads like this, "But the LORD watches over those who fear him, those who rely on his unfailing love" (And here comes the promise.) "He rescues them from death and keeps them alive in times of famine. We put our hope in the LORD. He is our help and our shield." (Psalm 33:18-20, NLT) This is a promise from God.

Our lives are filled with brokenness we didn't ask for. This world is filled with hurting people, and the grave is in the midst of it all. But God is on the other side, offering you a promise. A promise that through every circumstance, down every road, no matter the dark night, no matter if you can see him or if you're totally blind to his hand in your life—he promises you that he will deliver you through any circumstance, and his sovereign hand will carry you from any grave, out of every tomb, gather you from the dust of the air, and bring you into the very presence of his Son.

Look at how Psalm 46 reads; "Be still and know that I am God!" (Psalm 46:10, NLT) To be still simply means to stand right in the middle of the madness, right in the middle of the confusion, the chaos, the calamity, the unbelief, the death, the midnight, the prison, the sadness—to stand right in the middle of it and say, "God, I don't see what you're doing in this, but if it makes a difference in Heaven, I will stand still in the midst of it all, and I WILL WORSHIP YOU, GOD."[v]

MW

CHAPTER FIVE

GYM OF DREAMS

"Hello?" I answered.

"Yes, is this Drake?" the voice on the other end of the line asked.

"It is. How can I help you?"

"This is Brother Bill from Eagle Lake. I was calling to let you know we decided to go a different route. We love your preaching style, but because of your age, many church members have their concerns about hiring a twenty-one-year-old as our senior pastor."

"Okay, I understand. I hope you all find who it is you're looking for."

A few minutes went by until my phone rang again.

"Hello?"

"Hi, this is Mrs. Celeste. I was calling to tell you that Hepzibah decided to go a different direction. We really enjoyed your sermons, but because of your involvement with Seminary, we are concerned with your availability on a day-to-day basis. Because of that, we are not going to offer you the pastorate position."

"Okay," I replied, "I understand. Thank you for your consideration, and I hope you find the person that God has in store."

Hanging up the phone, I just sat there as the cold metal chair began to creep up my back.

I sat in silence for hours as Catherine was in the back room painting for one of our church member's restaurants. My plans of becoming a pastor had suddenly dissipated into nothingness.

"But why, God?" I asked. "You know how much I need the pay raise. I cannot make it on one hundred and eighty-four dollars and thirty-four cents per week. I need a house, gas, food—not to mention money to pay for school. God, I do not understand. Why is this happening?" *Discerning God's call is more of a relationship than a route; more about the journey than the destination.*

I sat there for the next two hours, asking the same questions over and over.

Catherine soon finished up painting and came up to the front. "Are you okay?" she asked.

"Yep, just fine."

She knew everything was not "just fine," but decided it was best not to talk about it. She is smart like that.

Before we started home, we had to run the paintbrushes back by the Sullivan's house, the owners of the restaurant, so Catherine ran in while I sat in the car.

Though the Sullivans are a sweet family, the tendency

to get long-winded runs in their blood, and I didn't have the emotional energy to engage in casual pleasantry.

A few minutes went by until Mr. Ken came outside walking towards my car. *Oh Lord, here we go. I'll be here forever.*

"Drake, how is life going?" Mr. Ken asked.

Of course, I told him everything was fine, just like I told Catherine. Honestly, I have a hard time opening up and telling people what is actually on my mind. I keep my walls up.

"Well, that's good. I don't know why I feel obliged to tell you this, but I need to get something off my chest."

"Okay!" He had my attention.

"Last year, I was fired from my job. I had a wife and two kids. Well, I didn't get fired; my business shut down, so I was unemployed. When that happened, I questioned God—a lot.

"After a few months of looking, I finally found a job that I was a shoo-in for. I knew everyone who worked there. I knew the managers. I had the experience; I thought this was where God wanted me. I applied, and two weeks later received a phone call saying they hired another person.

"Drake, I was so confused. I still am. But in the midst of it all, I felt a calling to start a restaurant. I have always wanted to since I was a child, so when the opportunity presented itself to buy a building, I talked to my wife, and we decided to go for it. I still don't know why or for what purpose yet. I don't know how we will make money until it opens, or if we will once it does. But I do know we are in the will of God. I don't know why I'm telling you this. I feel like you should know why I'm starting the restaurant, I guess.

"Sometimes Drake, I feel overwhelmed, stressed, and worried. But, somehow, in the midst of all the chaos, I have a sense of peace because I know I have a Savior who is guiding my steps. My family doesn't understand my calling yet. My sister doesn't even understand, and that hurts. They all tell me I've lost my mind, but that's okay. I know they don't see the vision yet because God hasn't given it to them the way he has given it to me."

GOD SEES, HEARS, AND CARES FOR YOU!

After he finished talking, I was speechless. I couldn't breathe. I was doing my best not to cry. To this day I have not told Mr. Ken what that conversation meant to me, (If you're reading this Mr. Ken, thank you for sharing) but it blew me up inside. Somehow, a guy whom I barely knew, told me exactly what I needed to hear at the time I needed to hear it. I remember thinking in that moment *"GOD SEES ME, HEARS ME, AND CARES FOR ME."* ***And GOD SEES, HEARS, AND CARES FOR YOU!***

PREPARED BUT PLIABLE

I love guns. Always have. For Christmas one year, when I was five, I dreamed of getting my first firearm. When Christmas morning came, to my surprise, I unwrapped an orange popgun.

"Ugghhhhhh. But Daddddddd. I want a real gun like you have."

For next year's Christmas, I wanted the same thing—but this time an actual gun! Dad told me he bought one, and I could tell it was real because of the wrapping. *"My dream has come true!"* I thought. Sad thing is, on Christmas morning I opened a Daisy BB gun.

"Dad. This is not what I meant by 'real gun.' I want one that goes 'BOOM,' like yours."

On a much more serious note, we have all been there—at the bedpost of broken dreams.

> *"Sometimes, to get your life back, you have to face the death of what you thought your life would look like."*

- Maybe something you worked so hard for went up in smoke.
- Maybe the life you envisioned was shot down.
- Or the job you applied for fell through.

Lysa TerKeurst, writing about her dating life, said, *"Sometimes, to get your life back, you have to face the death of what you thought your life would look like."* I think the same can be true of broken dreams. Ultimately, we need to walk somewhere between being *prepared but pliable*. Prepared meaning we do not need to live our lives flying by the seat of our pants, not planning for anything or preparing ourselves for the future. And pliable meaning able to adapt to changes that we didn't plan for. We need to have an agenda, go to school, prepare ourselves, organize, have a financial budget, even have an idea of where we want to work. But we also want to become flexible enough for God to move.

Genesis 37 teaches us as much. Let's jump into the text, starting in verse five.

5 (a) One-night Joseph had a dream,

I think I should sidebar here for a second and say that God is a dream giver. We talked earlier about our purpose in life, but along with purpose, God has given us a passion. Go for your passion! Whatever it is. Your passion may be business, engineering, law, missions, medicine—but don't let your passion supersede your purpose in it all. If your passion is to teach kids, do it in a way that brings glory to God. If your passion is in the arts, do it in a way that brings God glory. Colossians 3:17 says it this way; "And whatever you do, whether in word or deed, do it all in the name of the Lord Jesus, giving thanks to God the Father through him." (NIV)

Okay, back to the original text:

> 5 (b) *and when he told his brothers about it,*
> *they hated him more than ever.*

People will put down on your dreams. They will come alongside you and say, "You can't do it. You're not tall enough, smart enough, good enough." But be careful about who you let speak into your life. **If God has given you the dream, God will see you through it.** You can be whatever you want to be. Hard work and determination are worth more than talent and potential.

> 6 *"Listen to this dream," he said.*
> 7 *"We were out in the field, tying up bundles of grain. Suddenly my bundle stood up, and your bundles all gathered around and bowed low before mine!"*
> 8 *His brothers responded, "So you think you will be our king, do you? Do you actually think you will reign over us?" And they hated him all the more because of his dreams and the way he talked about them.*

Sidebar again—there is a correct way to tell people your ten-year-plan. When I attended Mississippi

College, there was a youth minister who came into class and told us that he dreamed of pastoring the biggest church in the world. There is nothing wrong with that passion, but he went on to tell us that he heard from God, and it was going to happen. I laughed and thought it was funny—but I say this to point as an illustration that sometimes, a good dream can be told in a bad way. And when that happens, people might get upset with you or just annoyed. So, be quick to listen and slow to speak. Joseph will learn this later on in his story.

> 9 Soon Joseph had another dream, and again he told his brothers about it. "Listen, I have had another dream," he said. "The sun, moon, and eleven stars bowed low before me!"
> 10 This time he told the dream to his father as well as to his brothers, but his father scolded him. "What kind of dream is that?" he asked. "Will your mother and I and your brothers actually come and bow to the ground before you?"
> 11 But while his brothers were jealous of Joseph, his father wondered what the dreams meant.
> 12 Soon after this, Joseph's brothers went to pasture their father's flocks at Shechem.
> 13 When they had been gone for some time, Jacob said to Joseph, "Your brothers are pasturing the sheep at Shechem. Get ready, and I will send you to them." (Don't miss these next few words.)
> "I'm ready to go," Joseph replied.

Joseph replied, "I'm ready." He was prepared. He didn't have everything, but he had what he needed.

His father said, "Get ready to go," and Joseph responded, "I'm already ready. I've been ready. I am prepared."

"How does that apply to me?" you ask. Simply put, get ready for God's calling. Go get the college degree that you need. Move to Atlanta to pursue your career in music. Work on the spreadsheet. Paint the new baby's room pink. Save money to buy the car. Think out ramifications of a decision. Plan your speech in the boardroom. Apply for your dream job. Prepare for things. But as you prepare, you also want to be pliable, and we are going to see that in Joseph's story as well.

Let's pick back up with verse 18:

18 When Joseph's brothers saw him coming, they recognized him in the distance. As he approached, they made plans to kill him. 19 "Here comes the dreamer!" they said.
20 "Come on, let's kill him and throw him into one of these cisterns. We can tell our father, 'A wild animal has eaten him.' Then we'll see what becomes of his dreams!"
21 But when Reuben heard of their scheme, he came to Joseph's rescue. "Let's not kill him," he said.
22 "Why should we shed any blood? Let's just throw him into this empty cistern here in the wilderness. Then he'll die without our laying a hand on him." Reuben was secretly planning to rescue Joseph and return him to his father.

Joseph was thrown into a pit and then his brothers sold him to some Egyptians—talk about turning a profit. And here is how the story concludes:

> 1 Now Joseph had been taken down to Egypt. Potiphar, an Egyptian who was one of Pharaoh's officials, the captain of the guard, bought him from the Ishmaelites who had taken him there.
> 2 The Lord was with Joseph so that he prospered, and he lived in the house of his Egyptian master.
> 3 When his master saw that the Lord was with him and that the Lord gave him success in everything he did,
> 4 Joseph found favor in his eyes and became his attendant. Potiphar put him in charge of his household, and he entrusted to his care everything he owned.

Now Joseph had never prepared to be a slave, much less to be an attendant to an Egyptian officer. But because he was pliable, God blessed Joseph in the middle of his situation. **Maybe you're two steps ahead and thinking, "God was preparing him all along to be a slave and an attendant," and to that, I would say, "Correct, but Joseph didn't know that. Joseph still had to be pliable, and the same is true for us."**

Later on, Potiphar's wife lied about Joseph, and because of this, Potiphar had him thrown in jail.

Now Joseph goes from a dreamer, to the pit, to Potiphar, and currently is in prison—but once again, Joseph was pliable. Joseph didn't want to be in jail, nor did he expect to be. But there he sat. And God used him to interpret people's dreams. *Joseph learned not to be a **dream proclaimer**, but **a dream giver**.*

Joseph never prepared for dream interpretations. He didn't take eighteen college credit hours to minor in dream interpretation, nor did he read book after book on 'how to interpret dreams?' In other words, Joseph wasn't prepared, but God used him because of his adaptability.

We see later in the story that Joseph was released from prison and brought into Pharaoh's palace to interpret a dream for him. And in that interpretation, Joseph's dream came true from all those years before. Pharaoh put Joseph in charge of all he had and he (Joseph) rescued the whole land from dying of famine.

Joseph went from the pit, to Potiphar, to prison, and ultimately, to the palace—but how? Because he was *prepared* by God *and pliable* from runt to ruler.

Gem of a Dream

We were a middle-class family growing up, so we rarely got to have big birthday parties. Typically, we just invited over family and ate some cake. However, for my eight-year-old birthday party, Mom said that we were going to rent out Gym of Dreams. She also gave me permission to invite all my friends. Now Gym of Dreams was *the* place to have birthday parties as a kid. They had a foam pit, (Hello, amazing to any eight-year-old.), trampolines, zip-lines, obstacle courses, and anything else that an eight-year-old would dream of.

I know what you may be thinking; "*Ahhh, I see where this is going; he is going to tell us of a broken dream and that he didn't get to go. Or this story is about to take a turn and talk about somebody breaking their leg.*" Well, actually no, thank you very much. I did get to have a birthday party there, and nobody got hurt, praise Jesus. In fact, my best friend, Will Jackson, and I watched the SEC basketball tournament when we should have been inside opening presents. But we have all gotten excited for a gem of a dream in our life that turned out to be a royal bust.

Most of us have been there before—excited about a door that opened only for us to take one step through the threshold and have it slammed in our face.

Take, for example, Billy Graham. He wanted to be a Chaplin in the Military, but in 1944 got denied due to being underweight. He was given some time to fatten up but then came down with the mumps and was denied again. I can hear Billy's prayer that night, "God, you're kidding me, right? I just want to make a difference for your kingdom. Why does it seem like you're against me?"

It is easy to question God when life falls apart and dreams crumble. The **LORD** sometimes crushes our dreams. Just look at David and the temple. David wanted to build a temple for the Lord but God told him "no." This may come as a shock, but **Satan** can also wreck our plans. For instance, Paul was trying to sail to Thessalonica to encourage the believers, but wrote a letter to them instead saying, "I, Paul, tried again and again, but was kept from coming to see you by Satan." (1 Thessalonians 2:18, NLT). Do not think that Satan controls your destiny, because God is ultimately sovereign over all things, but Satan certainly plays a roll.

God has more grace than a GPS.

Sometimes, the reason why your plans aren't working out is because of **YOU**. You messed up; you sinned; and now your path has altered course. But hear this! God has more grace than a GPS. When we take a wrong turn driving, Siri informs us that she is rerouting, but when it comes to God we think, *"I've screwed up. Now there is no way God will bless me."* But doesn't God give more grace than Siri?

Take the people in Samuel's day, for example. They asked Samuel for a king, but the LORD had already told them he would rule as their king. (See Samuel 8 and Deuteronomy 17:15)

After Samuel anointed Saul, the people realized their sin.

To chase a rabbit for a moment, sin has consequences. Don't over-look that! We sin, and that changes our plans. You planned on being married to the same person forever, but you cheated, so now they're gone. You planned on having the same job forever, but you lied, and now you're jobless. Look at Moses. He never got to enter the promised land. Instead, God buried him right outside its boundary. BUTTTTTTT God's plan prevailed through sin. Moses still entered the promised land, just years later on the Mountain of Transfiguration.

God still ruled as the Israelites' king. Just a few hundred years after Saul, when the King of Kings came.

Peter Syndrome

A few years ago, a new song came out that spread through the Church called "Church Clap." It was a Hip-Hop song, and there was a dance that could be done with it. Kenzie, one of the youth, taught me how to do it. Of course, I can't dance, so it took me all evening to learn, but I finally figured it out—or so I thought.

We had a county wide Epiphany Event where I encountered another youth group dancing to the song; incorrectly however, so I was quick to inform these "wannabe Michael Jacksons" on how it was supposed to be done. To my shock, they all busted out laughing. Nothing was funny to me! So I called Kenzie intending on getting her to explain the dance for these poor no-dancing souls. Giggling, Kenzie said, "Drake, I don't actually know how the dance goes. I just made something up." *Wow—now I look like a complete moron. Thanks, Kenz.*

I thought I knew the dance, but I was ignorant all along, and this is exactly how the Peter Syndrome works.

Peter thought Jesus was going to lead Israel out of bondage. Peter spent his early life hearing how the Messiah would one day lead Israel to be a great nation again. Now, in his mid-twenties, Peter was following the Anointed One. But when Jesus announced he was going to Jerusalem to die, Peter retorted, "Ummmmm, no buddy. You must not have read the Scriptures. You are not dying today, or tomorrow, or the next day; we have things to do and ain't nobody got time to be dying. So, you think you know what's going to happen, but I know better, and you dying isn't part of the plan." (And yes, I know that is bad grammer.)

The flip side of that is we can spend three years, as Peter did, or thirty years, totally investing our lives into a dream that instantly goes up in smoke. Our roof can cave in, and when that happens, it's easy to question God.

- "God, I thought she was the one."
- "God, I thought this was the job."
- "I don't understand; I thought you said...?"
- "Why am I being relocated to Pittsburg?"

Look at Paul's life. We touched on this idea a bit earlier, but Paul had a mission to preach the Gospel to all nations. This was his passion and purpose, but his plan got **put on hold** when he got **put in handcuffs** and taken to jail. Time and time again, he was sent to prison until, eventually, he was sentenced to house arrest for life.

However, although Paul didn't understand God's plan, there is no record of him showing symptoms of the Peter Syndrome questioning God. Instead, look what he writes:

1) Ephesians 6:12–*I am in chains now, still preaching this message as God's ambassador. So pray that I will keep on speaking boldly for him, as I should.*
2) Philippians 1:12-13–*And I want you to know, my dear brothers and sisters, that everything that has happened to*

me here has helped to spread the Good News. For everyone here, including the whole palace guard, knows that I am in chains because of Christ. And because of my imprisonment, most of the believers here have gained confidence and boldly speak God's message without fear.
3) Colossians 4:18–*Remember my chains. May God's grace be with you.*
4) 2 Timothy 1:8–*And don't be ashamed of me, either, even though I'm in prison for him.*
5) 2 Timothy 1:12–*That is why I am suffering here in prison. But I am not ashamed of it.*
6) Philemon 1:1–*This letter is from Paul, a prisoner for preaching the Good News about Christ Jesus, and from our brother Timothy. (NLT)*

Paul could have easily given up, handcuffed to the floor. But it was those very hands that wrote a third of the New Testament. In the brevity of life, it can be hard to find purpose in wasted years. Education and the idea of being intelligent are so highly valued in today's culture that we forget that God's ways are higher than our own.

The Peter Syndrome is contagious. It spreads in the air; by touch; by germs. It goes undetected until dreams break, and the symptoms become evident and deadly.

- **Here is the left hook,** "God's providence will prevail!"
- **Here is the call,** "Worship God through the fog of misunderstanding."

Remember the Mississippi State basketball game I

talked about earlier—the one Will and I watched when we should have been opening presents at Gym of Dreams? Here is what a reporter wrote about the final shot that forced overtime in that game:

"The clock starts when the shooter catches the ball, on the left wing, twenty-four feet from the basket. Two seconds left. He has run off a screen from the baseline, so his momentum carries him toward midcourt. He pushes hard off his right foot and pivots back to the left. One-point-four seconds. When he rises off the floor, the force of this hard cut is still carrying him left. One second. He believes Jesus will guide this shot.

"The shooter flicks his right wrist at the peak of his jump, and if you photographed him now, you could put it in a textbook. Eight tenths of a second. The ball is still airborne when time expires and the horn sounds. The shot is almost perfect. But the shooter was drifting left, as you recall, and the ball lands just left of the target. It hits the back of the rim, the boxy part with the springs, and the springs rattle. The ball caroms from back rim to front, seeming to gain speed as it goes, and it suddenly leaps out of the cylinder.

"The secret things belong unto the Lord our God. The shooter believes this because his Bible says so, and because of what he has seen. Soon he will believe it more deeply than ever. The ball sails toward the backboard, hits the center of the white square, and falls through the net.

"This shot does nothing to change the game's outcome. Mississippi State still won. And yet, for pure utility, it may be as great as any play in the history of sports. Eight minutes later, during the Southeastern Conference tournament game between Alabama and Mississippi State, a tornado roared through downtown Atlanta, hovering right over the dome housing the SEC tournament. By morning, Alabama's point guard, Mykal Riley's, three-pointer was known as The Shot That Saved Lives. If it had not been for that shot, I don't even want to think of the lives that would have been lost."

That game is a crazy story of God's providence. It saturated me with all kinds of emotions. The moment the shot landed, I was so angry. When the shot crossed through the iron, my dreams of winning outstretched my heart's desire. I was distraught. But eight minutes later, my reality was given new perspective. My dreams got reshaped from something as infinitesimal as a silly basketball game to the lives of thousands.

> Be careful not to abort God's plan for a good one.

I don't like the idea that my dreams will fall through the cracks of expectation and neither do you, but at all costs, I want to avoid the Peter Syndrome. I will be careful not to abort **God's plan** for a **good one** because right around the corner might stand the salvation of hundreds. The moment I press the eject button on God's plans and parachute safely to my own desires I become my own captain journeying to shipwreck.

Irreducible Minimum II

We talked about the irreducible minimum a few pages ago—but what is the irreducible minimum for a Christian? When everything else is taken away, what is left? To ask it differently, "What is most important?" It is a great question to ask, but revolutionary to answer. My answer is, "Being with God." However, you must answer that question for yourself. I want to conclude this chapter, by pointing us to some Old Testament Scriptures that will aid in finding our answer.

God told Moses on Mt. Sinai *"Get going, you and the people you brought up from the land of Egypt. Go up to the land I swore to give to Abraham, Isaac, and Jacob. I told them, 'I will give this land to your descendants.' And I will send an angel before you to drive out the Canaanites, Amorites, Hittites, Perizzites, Hivites, and Jebusites. Go up to this land that flows with milk and honey. But I will not travel among you, for you are a stubborn and rebellious people. If I did, I would surely destroy you along the way."* (Exodus 33:1-3, NLT)

Moses didn't like that idea, so he responded to God, "I will not go without you. If you don't go with us, let us stay here forever" (Exodus 33:15, NLT). For Moses, to take the land was **not** the irreducible minimum; it was something he could live without. God's presence, on the other hand, could not be absent. It was something that Moses would not sacrifice, and so it is in our lives.

To say it a bit differently, Moses could have replied, "God, thank you for giving me everything that our ancestors have longed for. Thank you for giving us victory over our enemies. Thank you for delivering us out of Egypt. I even thank you for the grace you have already bestowed on our behalf. But, if you're not coming, I'm out. I am staying right here, at the base of the mountain, because to be in a desert with you is better than an oasis apart."

To be in a desert with you is better than an oasis apart.

To apply that to your life, God might give you the job you want, a beautiful house, a great wife, a good life, obedient children, good health, and all the while not be with you. And to that, I would suggest saying to God, "No thanks, I want you; wherever that is."

So, in the middle of broken dreams and unanswered prayers, it may be that we are in the desert, but with God. We might be in the pit, but with God. We might be in the psych ward but with God. We might be in the trenches but with God. Anxiety might attack, but we are with God. We may be wondering around in the empty tomb, but in that tomb, in that fire, in that jail, in that storm, God is present.

Let me conclude by sharing the second half of Joseph's story.

Pharaoh elevated Joseph to second-in-command of all Egypt with the task of storing up enough food for the coming famine. Once the famine struck, his

> **Joseph followed his God and then his dreams followed him.**

brothers journeyed over to Egypt from Israel to ask for rations. Little did they know, their brother would be the one handing them out.

After two decades, Joseph's dreams had now come true. But is the story of Joseph about him following his dreams? Absolutely not! Joseph followed his God and then his dreams followed him. The story of Joseph is not, "Joseph had a dream, and he held on really tight to his dream."

I used to think the story was all about Joseph's perseverance. I have even preached sermons with the motif, "Joseph had a dream! Do you have a dream? Follow your dream!" But that's not really what the story is all about. And that is not what your story is all about either.

Your irreducible minimum is not following your heart's desires nor following your dreams. They may die or change over time. Your irreducible minimum is following your God.

Follow Jesus Christ! And his dreams will follow you!

MW

INTERLUDE

THE STORY CONTINUES

"Silas, look!" Paul exclaimed as a crack went streaking down the wall.

Turning, Silas stumbled backward, but the floor chains dug into his wrist making their presence felt.

"Are you thinking what I'm thinking?"

"IT'S AN EARTHQUAKE! I THINK IT'S AN EARTHQUAKE!" one of the prisoners shouted.

The jailer sprinted down dodging bits of concrete as it fell from the roof.

Click. Click. Click. Click. Click.

The sound of the jailer's footsteps could be heard as he walked around.

"Is that what I think it is?" asked the jailer to his lesser aide. "Are all the prison doors open?"

"Yes sir. It looks that way, sir."

The jailer drew his sword and put it to his neck. The dullness of the blade caused a slight hesitation. But after all, his life was over.

"Stop! Don't do it! We're all still here," he heard from the inner stall.

Grabbing a torch, the jailer made his way around the prison floor. One by one, he visited each stall containing inmates completely unshackled with the doors swung wide open.

"Sirs," the jailer asked approaching the stall holding Paul and Silas, "What must I do to be saved? I heard your singing from the upper room, and it's obvious the God you serve has answered your prayers."

(If you're asking yourself the same question as the jailer, take heed to Paul's response.) "Believe in the Lord Jesus, and you will be saved." (Acts 16:31, NIV)

Around two o'clock in the morning, the jailer invited Paul and Silas to his home.

"Let me grab a bowl of water, and a damp rag to clean those wounds," the jailer offered as they walked in. "You both can sit here in the kitchen. I'll be right back. The water well is just around the corner."

When the jailer returned, he began to suture up Paul's right eye. Meanwhile, Silas asked if he had thought anymore about their earlier conversation.

Wringing out the bloody rag by twisting it, he responded, "I have. But just who is this Jesus character you're speaking of?"

"Hmmm, good question. You see, Jesus is the Son of..."

"Hold up one second. Let me go get my family before you start explaining everything. I want them to hear this!"

Immediately, the jailer went and fetched his family. While everyone gathered around, Paul and Silas explained the Gospel of Jesus, who he was, and why he died.

"What do you all think about Jesus? Do you believe what I am telling you?" asked Paul.

Nodding to indicate they did, Paul began to tell the story of Jesus's baptism. "We want to be baptized, too!" exclaimed the jailer's family.

"Well then. Let's get you all baptized."

And just like that, a new family of believers was added to the kingdom of God. And it all came on the brink of an earthquake.

MW

CHAPTER SIX

A DIFFERENT KIND OF EARTHQUAKE

Growing up, I never got into professional basketball much. I always thought there were too many fouls called, and to some extent, I still do. As I got older, however, I began to love watching the Golden State Warriors.

Now, as for playing basketball, I am terrible. I would probably rank myself somewhere in the top ten world's worst basketball players. Consequently, when people ask me how I became a fan, I really don't have an answer. To be honest, I don't know if there is a perfect starting point, but I guess it all began in college.

My roommate at the time was a guy by the name of Braxton Hinton, who just so happened to be my doubles partner in tennis and my best friend.

Our typical day wasn't much different than any other college student's: wake up, get breakfast, go to class, eat lunch, take a power nap, wake up in time for tennis, practice for three hours, then spend the rest of our evening on the campus driving range grinding for our green jackets.

Most nights, we would come in from golf and watch whatever football game that was on TV. But one day, undenounced to us, we lost our TV remote. We looked everywhere in that hundred-square-foot dorm but could never find it. Eventually, we came to the conclusion that it grew legs, got up, and walked off.

Anyways, our television was stuck on one channel for the remainder of the year, but thankfully it was the greatest channel to ever be stuck with: ESPN. At least during football season it was the champion channel choice, but then came basketball season. I would have turned it a million times over if I could have, but nope—no remote. So there I sat, watching basketball most every night as I fell asleep.

Remarkably, the more I watched it, the more I began to like it. I hated to admit it, especially to myself, but basketball was growing on me. Many nights consisted of me staying up late just to ogle Steph Curry hit threes from the timeline. I was in love, and my bride-to-be was the Golden State Warriors.

I'll never forget the first NBA finals I watched. I found one of my worn-out, white T-shirts and decorated it with a red Sharpie marker. I still have that shirt by the way. I'll wear it from time to time when I need to bring back the good luck mojo. Scratch that—*excellent* luck mojo.

A few months after the wreck, one of my best friends, Blake Smith, found out about the difficulties that I was walking through and decided to buy us two tickets to a Warriors game in San Francisco. He had extra airfare mileage points, so I was able to fly gratis. (I know, I know, I am blessed to have such a generous friend.)

Of course, I took him up on his offer.

It was a Thursday night in February when we boarded a plane and headed to the West Coast.

The game wasn't until Saturday evening, and—to my surprise—Blake already had our weekend planned.

Friday morning came, and we loaded a bus which took us on a rolling tour through the city. We were able to see the Painted Ladies (also known as the "Full House" houses), Coit Tower, and the Golden Gate Bridge. Then we got the chance to walk down Lombard Street and explore a few Cathedrals. Our adventure eventually took us through China Town where we saw the only place in the world that makes homemade fortune cookies.

Of course, before we left, I had to grab Catherine a souvenir—her favorite plant, a succulent.

The next morning, we caught an Uber to Golden Gate Park where we rented bicycles and biked from Sixth Avenue to the ocean—about a three-mile journey. *Beep. Beep.*

We saw everything from redwood trees to buffalos.

On our bike ride over, I debated on whether I would jump into the ocean or not. I had never swum in an ocean before—only a gulf. So when I finally made up my mind, I went running out into the crashing waves. Keep in mind it was mid-February and about forty-three degrees outside. I froze my tail off! There was no one else in the ocean besides surfers in thermal suits and me—swimming around half-dressed. In hindsight, probably not a great idea, but you only live once.

For reasons concerning wet clothes and males, I left my attire on the beach for the bike ride back. *What did I wear on the way to the bike shop,* you may wonder? My underwear, of course. It's California, anything goes! No, I am just kidding. I had an extra pair of shorts with me.

That evening, as we headed to Oracle Arena, Blake and I slowly tried to incorporate Christianity into our conversations with the Uber driver. Wanting to change the topic of discussion, the driver began to ask about our jobs. To this, I mentally deliberated, *GOTCHA. I am a youth pastor. Back to the Jesus conversation buddy*. But when I told him what I did for a living, he informed us that he was an Earthquake-ologist. That's what I will call him anyway. Just know that he was really into earthquakes, which was the reason, he later revealed, for moving to San Francisco in the first place.

Searching for a conversation toehold (I guess) or just uncomfortable with the awkward silence that was in the car, he went on to tell us how earthquakes were measured.

"See, earthquakes are measured by moment magnitude, which is based on the seismic movement of the earthquake. This is equal to the shear modulus of the rock near the fault multiplied by the average amount of slip on the fault and the size of the area that slipped."[i] (And yes, I had to use Google to spell those words.)

"Can you speak English, buddy?" I responded.

A DIFFERENT KIND OF EARTHQUAKE

"Basically, it measures how much the earth quakes during an earthquake."

"Thank you—much better."

So, as he is telling us all this, I asked him when the last earthquake he experienced was.

Laughing, I suppose because he knew he was about to blow our minds, he replied, "About fifteen minutes ago. I get alerts on my phone when the seismograph gets a significant reading."

Seeing that his dream of blowing our minds had just come to fruition, he went on to explain, "Yeah, see, earthquakes happen in San Francisco every day. It's just seldom that we actually feel them. Each year in Southern California, there are over ten-thousand earthquakes that get measured. However, less than one percent can even be felt."

My heart began to beat fast in my chest! I didn't know whether to be excited that I had experienced an earthquake or terrified of the fact that I had without the knowledge of it.

So why do I tell this story? Why do I tell you about my Golden State Warrior obsession, and my trip to San Fran from several years ago? Especially on a night like tonight, because as I am typing, the Warriors just lost Game Six to the Raptors in the NBA Finals. A slight depression is setting in. But does telling you all this have a point? Yes!

See, earthquakes work similarly in our lives. Though we are talking about a different kind of earthquake, they occupy the same space.

Not every earthquake that comes will shake the foundations of your prison. Nor will it, in every circumstance, break the chains of bondage. In fact, most earthquakes that occur in the midnight will never even crack the Richter scale. In other words, the earthquake that comes for you won't always deliver you from pornography, selfishness, or addiction. It won't change the circumstances of your marriage. And please understand this; it won't undo the past five years of your life. But in every situation in which you worship God, an earthquake will happen, either in Heaven or on Earth.

> In every situation in which you worship God, an earthquake will happen, either in Heaven or on Earth.

When I originally typed this statement, I didn't think twice about it. But as I began to read over and make corrections, I spent two weeks debating on whether or not this statement was true. I had to ask myself the difficult question—"*will God make his presence felt, whether in deliverance, or strength to endure, or courage to keep moving forward, or wisdom? Or will I walk through life and, for periods of time, wonder where God is and why he hasn't responded?*"

A DIFFERENT KIND OF EARTHQUAKE

But then I realized that question was the whole reason I wrote this chapter, and the answer is *yes*. See, there will come times when God goes unseen and unfelt. There will come times during our worship when we feel nothing—no earthquake coming to save us, no walls that come tumbling down freeing us from our financial debt or our character flaws. But when nothing is felt, it doesn't mean that nothing is there. When we don't see God, it doesn't mean that he isn't present. After all, look at what Scripture says: "Now faith is confidence in what we hope for and assurance about what we do not see" (Hebrews 11:1, NIV). "So we fix our eyes not on what is seen, but on what is unseen, since what is seen is temporary, but what is unseen is eternal" (2 Corinthians 4:18, NIV).

I think it's crucial not to sweep anything under the rug here. To come alongside this idea and say, sometimes the prayer doesn't get answered. Sometimes thoughts of suicide, depression, fear, or anxiety don't cease. In fact, sometimes they keep coming even stronger, and we are left to endure one more day. Sometimes we don't have an answer and don't see the light at the end of the tunnel. However, though we do not see every blessing God sends, the flip side of the initial question is true as well. God **is** giving us strength in the midnight. God **is** moving, **is** communicating, and **is** giving to us all the days of our life.

But how do I know that is true? How do I know God is sending when I can't feel it? When I can't see it? Well, spiritually speaking, because Scripture tells us as much.

MORNING IN DOTHAN

Just look at the story of Elisha. He was quickly approached by his young servant; "Sir, there is an army surrounding us with every intention to kill us."

Elisha looked down towards his aide and said, "Greater is the number on our side than on theirs."

The young man replied, "What? It's just me and you here, sir. There is an army on the hillside!"

Elisha looked up to Heaven and prayed, "LORD, please open his eyes." And here is how Scripture reads in response: "The LORD opened the young man's eyes, and when he looked up, he saw that the hillside around Elisha was filled with horses and chariots of fire" (2 Kings 6:17, NLT).

And this is what I think needs to happen to us. This whole idea of praying, "Lord, please open my eyes. I know I cannot see an earthquake all that well right now. And I know that I have some enemies marching against me on the hillside. And you know that I am in a midnight that I can't see my way out of. And to be honest Lord, I don't see you all too well right now either. So, if you would, could you please help me see?"

The servant wasn't blind before Elisha prayed. Physically speaking, he probably had better eyesight than Elisha. But Elisha had the ability to see God at work.

God was sending. God was giving. God was protecting. There is more to life than that which meets the eye. Going back to our initial question, *Can we know that God is sending when we can't feel it?*

Perhaps this story will shed some light:

One Sunday morning, an older gentleman walked down to the front of church during the invocation and asked the pastor if he could say a few words. Hesitant, the pastor agreed to let the man speak, so he addressed the crowd as follows:

"I have never stepped foot inside a church before. My wife has been a Christian for quite some time now and has frequently asked me to come with her to different church events. Eventually, to get her to stop nagging me, I gave in.

"I told Sherry before we came that the only way I would believe in Jesus was if someone did pushups in the aisle. If that happened, I would believe there was a God.

"Well, during the last night of the conference, there was a young man who walked down the aisle and began to do pushups. Instantly, I thought there was some colluding going on, so I asked my wife about it. I was suspicious that she had relayed the information to the pastor or to someone else, and that was the cause of the pushups. I accused her of doing such. But, of course, she denied it.

"I then became curious about this *pushups-in-the-aisle guy*. It took a while, but I eventually mustered up enough courage to call and confront him about the night at the leadership conference.

"I guess he could tell that I was a bit skeptical, however, this is what he communicated to me:

'I felt like the Spirit of God was telling me to walk down the aisle during every session and do pushups, but I didn't. I was worried about what others would think. Then a story came to mind about a Bible character who did something crazy for the kingdom of God—Phillip and the Ethiopian if you know the story. So eventually, I went down and did pushups.'

"His answer did it for me," the older man told the church.

"The reason I came down today is to tell you all, 'I believe in Jesus.' "

The audience all stood up in applause for this man coming to faith. But think about how differently that story could have ended.

There was a time for the *pushups-in-the-aisle guy* when he didn't know why God placed on his heart the obligation to go all "Rocky Balboa" in church. He didn't see any fruit from being obedient. He probably felt kind of foolish or maybe even embarrassed that he followed God. There might have even come a time where he questioned if it actually was God speaking to him in the first place. That is, until a few weeks later, when he was approached by a total stranger asking about the pushups.

Through the next few moments of conversation with the older gentleman, he got to see the *why* behind God's request. But that is often not the case.

A DIFFERENT KIND OF EARTHQUAKE

We don't always get to see the why. We don't always get to feel the earthquake. Nevertheless, there always is one.

Sometimes when the earth quakes, a life is changed due to our worship. People come up and ask, "What must I do to be saved?"

But other times when we worship, people look at us and say, "Shut up. You are in jail. WE ARE IN JAIL! This is a God-free zone, so shut up. There is no worship down here."

And if that is what they say, then God bless them—literally. But don't let anyone deter you from worshipping.

PONDERING YOUR THOUGHTS?

Today, one of my high school friend's one-week-old baby had a seizure. Seizures this early in a child's life cause brain damage that could affect the baby's later development. She doesn't know what the future holds for this baby, but right now she is holding her child in her arms.

I think to myself, *Will there be an earthquake in her life? Will God break in? What if she worships during the hardest moments of life? Does that make for an earthquake?* I picture someone like her reading this chapter and just thinking, *Yeah right. God is not coming into my circumstance. He hasn't changed anything for me in years, so why would he now?*

Have you ever been there? Maybe you're there now. It can be comforting to know that many times when

Paul was put into prison, an earthquake did not come for him either. In fact, the history of the Church states that Paul died in prison. But even when the earthquake did not come, *a different kind of earthquake* came. Paul writes, "And *because of my imprisonment,* most of the believers here have gained confidence and boldly speak God's message without fear" (Philippians 1:14, NLT).

So even though you don't see the walls breaking down, know that God has a plan in it all, and he is working all things for your good. I don't think this is the main point of the text, but it is worth noting that other peoples' chains fell off besides Paul's and Silas's.

> **Even when the earthquake did not come, *a different kind of earthquake* came.**

Paul and Silas weren't running around the prison saying, "Ha, look at us! We are free. We are out of here, suckers. The best of luck to you!"

No—everyone was set free. Paul and Silas had a captive audience in their prison, and so do you. When you choose to send up praises to God, it will change your life, yes, but it also has the capacity to break others out of their prison.

So, to my friend whose baby you hold right now, wondering what the future might hold, asking, "Will the seizures ever cease?" I say:

> There is no night too dark for a God who knows the dark side of the tomb.

"You might never see the blessing. You may never feel the ground shake—but don't let that frighten you. Heaven is looking down on you, smiling. Pray that God will open your eyes. God hears your prayers. He knows your heart.

"Your tears are a constant reminder to me.

"If it has been a few years now, I hope that life finds you well. And if you just so happen to find yourself reading this, know there is no night too dark for a God who knows the dark side of the tomb. Your earthquake will come! Your earthquake has come! Your earthquake may go M.I.A., but *a different kind of earthquake* is just around the corner!"

MW

CHAPTER SEVEN

ROOM OF MENTAL HEALTH—OR NOT-SO-MENTAL HEALTH

This was the last chapter I penned. In fact, I began it only five days before I turned in the final manuscript to the publishing company. Not because I didn't have anything to say on the subject matter, but because I did. I just didn't want to uncover my own issues, deal with my own problems. To quote Anne Lamott, "My mind is a bad neighborhood that I try not to go in alone."

A lot of people talk about their mental health from a perfect or completed tense, always speaking of it through the lens of the past. I know why people do this. As time goes on, understanding and wisdom become clearer and an image is presented of what they experienced. Afterall, the bottom of the valley doesn't offer the clearest view.

This may disqualify me from the conversation, but I want to offer my perspective from somewhere between the bottom and the mountaintop. Even as I type, I am getting over a spout of anxiety. Muscles in my back are tensed. My bones ache. Sleep has been like a drug the last few days. When these moments come, how can I get through them? What is the best way to manage life?

To some degree, I don't think it ever goes away. I am convinced that it is here to stay. That I will always struggle with worry, fear, anxiety, spouts of mental breakdown. And perhaps that is okay! Does a soldier ever leave the battlefield? Yet life marches on.

Perhaps this, too, is a lie. I will get better! I will persevere!

Before we get too far into this chapter, I think it is important to say that I don't want to relate in such a way that doesn't fully depict my life. I have never battled severe depression, nor do I pretend to know what life-altering anxiety feels like. I have only scratched the surface of these mental illnesses.

For instance, from my early childhood, I have been a pessimist. The negative view is easier to envision. Worry comes up from behind. From in front. From beside me. Worst case scenarios ransack my imagination. My mother walks into the grocery store, and within minutes I begin to mentally deliberate, *"somebody has robbed the store, stolen Mom. She is probably being wheeled off right now. De Facto, she is probably dead."*

As a young boy hunting alone in the woods, thoughts crept into my imagination when Dad and I departed: *"what if he gets bitten by a snake? What if he falls from his stand?"* Every coyote howl sent a thousand other embodiments of mental clutter for me to sort through and manage. I hated hunting alone. But I would have never told my father that. Stepping into manhood comes at a price. Fear must be overcome. But is it ever truly overcome?

Now that I think about it, today most all of my problems stem from a worst-case scenario mindset. *What if? What if? What if?*

I never realized how close to the edge I was until I fell. I never realized that any thought or scenario could send me into the pitfall. Any second I could come eyeball to eyeball with the existential horrors that only lie dormant within my mind. I never knew how close I was to self-implosion until I turned twenty.

Turning twenty a century past the roaring twenties is difficult. Could it be just as the Great Depression lay on the other side of such a luxurious decade of advancement and technology that a Great Depression could lie on the other side of ours? Except this one not taking out the stock market or closing down banks, but something much more important—our minds. "The price for being intelligent enough to be the first species to be fully aware of the cosmos might just be a capacity to feel a whole universe's worth of darkness." – Matt Haig

Darkness.

Darkness.

Darkness.

Midnight.

Midnight.

I hate the midnight! Anxiety won't let me sleep through it. So there I lie. Midnight. Midnight. Midnight.

"*Mockingbird. Be like a Mockingbird,*" I tell myself.

It's hard to see past the fog, to see anything objectively. We see the whole world through our corneas. We ourselves act as our only reference point.

Depression, anxiety, fear, A.D.D. (Attention Deficit Disorder), worry, O.C.D. (Obsessive-Compulsive Disorder), all affect people differently. There is no standard.

Thank God I have never walked through deep depression, but I pity the one who does. To be attacked by your own mind. No thank you. But nobody chooses depression, do they?

No.

Instead, it just happens. Out of the blue. You are in bed, and can't get out, can't go out in public, mind racing. Numbness creeps around your body like a spider web in the early morning light. That is my worst nightmare. But yet, I'm living in a version of it.

To most people, I look my usual self. Perhaps a bit more lethargic than normal, but inside, my mind can't rest.

I have tried several things to help; Baclofen, Prozac. Most recently I tried Adderall. I am scared to take them, even though they help. I don't want to become hooked. All these have been prescribed by my doctor, but nevertheless, addicts don't intend on becoming addicts.

Of course, I'm not saying don't take medicine. Do as you wish. But I am and always have been scared of the long-term effects that medicine will have. Especially medicine that affects the chemical balances in my brain. It's not a risk I'm willing to take. But if the depression got bad enough, I suppose I would do most anything for help.

Depression lies. It tells you there is no light at the end of the tunnel. It tells you your life is meaningless. It tells you life is not worth living. But depression itself is not a lie. It can be the most real thing you have ever experienced. It sinks its teeth in and won't let go. Yet no one can see it. Maybe they can see symptoms of it. But unlike a broken bone, depression can't be seen through an X-ray.

When I first fell into a state of indifference coupled with anxiety, I felt alone. Alone in my head. Left to dwell in my thoughts and afterthoughts. Although I was surrounded with surface level things like studies and sports and conversation, I was an island. Truth be told, I could have been surrounded by thousands of others and I would have still felt alone. I think that is one of the things that depression lies about.

Hopelessness wasn't a symptom of mine. I did and still do see a light at the end of the tunnel. But my tunnel walls are filled with to-do lists. One thing after another. A never-ending sequence of events guiding to my light. So, in essence, the light can be seen but never attained.

Panic on the other hand, is as real for me as life itself. I get it, honestly. My mom is an Olympic Gold Medalist when it comes to worrying. But panic goes even deeper than worry. Worry is a stepping stone that leads to something much darker.

I worry that I upset people on accident. I worry that I won't succeed. I worry that I will say the wrong thing. I worry about not being thankful enough. I worry that God sees me the way I see myself. I worry that I will lose everything I cherish. I even worry about not worrying—becoming nonchalant. I worry about becoming melodramatic. I worry about my brothers not loving me. I worry about who I see in the mirror. I worry about things I can't fix, and about things I can.

But then I panic.

I turn on a Podcast and the panic grows. Then, by outputting silence, my mind takes on a slew of information.

Outcome—my mind is baited and ready to be ransacked by the deepest darkness known to man—self-implosion.

Panic is actually there to help us. It is our body's way of telling us to do something. Fight or flight. So why does my mind take what is good and produce something so evil?

These attacks have gone by different names over the years; panic attack, nervous breakdown, mental breakdown, burnout—currently it goes by the name anxiety attack.

Our culture is set up to produce nervous people. The way our news and media outlets are designed are all based upon panic. The more terrifying the news, the higher the ratings.

ROOM OF MENTAL HEALTH—OR-NOT-SO-MENTAL-HEALTH

Business and sales do the same thing. Most every advertisement is geared towards showing you something you lack which they can provide. Could it be that in a climate of abundance we constantly feel in want or in need? I wouldn't call it getting better, but the moment I realized other people have it worse off than I do was at a party with the Mississippi College tennis team. Not that I cared to go to any of their so-called "parties," but there was a girl there I had a crush on, so I went.

Typically, parties make me feel uncomfortable. Especially when I am dealing with spouts of anxiety or mental fatigue. A party is the last place I want to be. It further implements my sense of aloneness in the world. However, getting out of my comfort zone and being social did help me. It brought a sense of belonging and even happiness. Maybe it wasn't the party that brought that feeling but the acceptance I often felt afterwards.

One night, a guy by the name of Maximillian came up to me after having his twelfth shot of Rum and asked, "Drake, why don't you ever drink? I don't understand! Everybody else here does."

He flew over from Germany the semester before I arrived but had never been introduced to the Gospel or to Church. All he knew was Humanism. We had grown close over the long, hot summer days of practice, so that night I explained who Jesus was. (As an aside, I think people can come to know Christ in all different states of mind. Being wasted isn't the most opportune moment to share Christ, but hey, worth a shot.)

He was pretty drunk, so I don't think he understood much, but he asked again why I didn't drink. This time, I gave him a more honest answer, "I come from a long line of people who can't go a day without drinking. My grandfather, his father before him, and probably his father. I don't want to become addicted." I think this offered him a bit more satisfaction. If not that, he at least understood and responded by saying, "Ahhhh. Yessssss. Now I understand you a bit more. You choose not to drink out of fear."

Being sinful, his acceptance of my answer caused the dopamine in my brain to spike, so I stayed silent even though his inference was not totally correct. I felt called by God not to drink—like John the Baptist and Samson. For me to drink would have been sin; though this is not true for everyone. But then he told me why he drank; "To have one (heck) of a good time."

I wanted to peel the onion, so I asked him to explain. I will never forget the next three minutes of our conversation. Max and I got real. He told me how alcohol is his escape.

Drinking is what he grew up believing to be the pinnacle of existence. Each moment was built to lead to a good time. But when he found this to be a lie, and that he was left empty, alcohol was his only way out. An escape from trying to escape.

I don't know why, but something about that night put life into a new perspective. Afterall, isn't life a perspective? Our perspective?

And my perspective changed that night: *At least when I struggle, I struggle with Jesus. I couldn't imagine struggling without him!*

Depression and Suicide

Depression is equivalent to walking around on hot coals. It affects everyone differently. *Pain is felt in different ways and to different degrees. It evokes different responses.*[i]

Mental illness is not biased. It comes after us all—the rich, the poor, the sick, the healthy, the attractive, and the not-so-attractive.

Matt Haig, in his book *Reasons to Stay Alive*, which I would encourage you to read if you are dealing with depression, anxiety, or suicide, as it certainly helped me, says this:

> "Suicide is in places including the UK and US a leading cause of death, accounting for over one in a hundred fatalities. According to figures from the World Health Organization, it kills more people than stomach cancer, cirrhosis of the liver, breast cancer, and Alzheimer's. Depression through self-harm kills more people than most other forms of violence warfare, terrorism, domestic abuse, assault, gun crime—put together.
>
> "Even more staggeringly, depression is a disease so bad that people are killing themselves because of it in a way they do not kill themselves with any other illness. Yet people still don't think depression really is that bad. If they did, they wouldn't say the things they say."[ii]

For the first time in over sixty years, the average life expectancy in the United States is going down.[iii] One of the leading contributing factors: suicide. It is the biggest killer of women and men between the ages of twenty and thirty-four.[iv] So why don't we take depression more seriously?

There is a fine line between being stressed out and actually being ill.

Just like anything else, depression has levels. Some cases are easy to identify. Others, not so much. Not because it doesn't feel bad or doesn't hurt—it does—but because the hurt and pain seems unrecognizable.

Here are some symptoms of depression:

- suffering from a constant restlessness
- a sense of dread
- feeling constantly "on edge"
- difficulty concentrating
- low self-esteem
- irritability
- impatience
- being easily distracted
- dizziness
- drowsiness and tiredness
- pins and needles
- irregular heartbeat (palpitations)
- muscle aches and tension
- dry mouth
- excessive sweating

- shortness of breath
- stomachache/nausea
- diarrhea
- headache
- loss of appetite
- excessive thirst
- frequent urinating[v]

Why do we get depressed? Why do we deal with anxiety? I think it has to do with unrationalized expectations. Just think about the reward for achieving a goal. Your reward is to set a new goal. And then another. And then another. Until you don't achieve one. Or die trying. Not only that, but with great power comes greater responsibility. So, because we have been given so much freedom and opportunity, expectations have output the essentials of life—food, sleep, prayer, sanity, relationships of any meaning. Just the fact that you are holding this book puts you in the top one percent of all human beings to ever live. Think about that! You are in the top one percentile of the most privileged people ever just by being able to read and own this book—any book for that matter.

But when depression strikes, none of that matters. Not because we don't want to be grateful or objective, but because nothing truly matters when depression strikes. Not our family. Not our looks. Not our job. Nothing! It's not that we don't care enough to think on these things—we do! It's just that thinking spirals the depression even further down.

ROOM OF MENTAL HEALTH—OR-NOT-SO-MENTAL-HEALTH

When suicide climbs through the crevasses of people's imagination, it's not that they want to die. It's that they don't want to live. People who take their own life still fear death. Just not as much as they fear living one more moment.[vi]

Take for instance the words of Elijah when he said; "I have had enough, Lord. Take my life." Or the other seven cases of suicide in the Bible: Abimelech, the prophet Ahithophel after betraying David, Zimri who burned himself alive, Saul and his armor bearer, Samson, and Jesus' disciple Judas.

Some people even say Jesus felt depressed and suicidal in Gethsemane the night before he was crucified. I don't know that I would say that; though Scripture says he was tempted in every way. But I do know what the author of Hebrews says, "For the joy that was set before him, Jesus endured the cross." To which I say, "Amen. Thank you, Jesus!" Because what that tells me is that I don't always have to put my best foot forward. Or maybe I do, but my best foot may be crippled. Afterall, if you take the crutch away from a lame person, he will still walk with a limp.

It tells me that it's okay to walk with a limp.

It tells me I don't always have to fake a smile. That there is a level to life called enduring. That Jesus knew what it felt like not to be a hundred percent. That I don't have to wish my way through life.

It tells me that I can talk to others and be honest with God. "Yeah. I'm not okay today. I am struggling.

Depression has me by the neck. I don't like it. I don't know how I'm going to make it through. I can't see through the fog. All I can see is the darkness. But I will endure through the end. I will persevere!"

When I was dealing with the aftermath of the wreck, I was mentally in a bad place. A terrible place. Sometime during the frustration, I came across this phrase by Levi Lusko that helped me find hope and perhaps it will help you; "I told God if he wanted me to walk with a limp for the rest of my life, I would, but if he healed me, I would not fake one."[vii]

I sometimes feel like my brain is a phone with too many apps open. This is why Adderall helps. It makes my mind organize thought patterns. It enables me to focus. To let go of the worry and use that mental power towards yielding something productive.

When mental lapses of stress and fear come, I try tons of things to help. Not that I'm actually trying to get better. These things just come as a byproduct to worry. I try to read. I try to catch up on my schoolwork. I sleep. I watch Netflix. I listen to podcasts. I play golf. I critique others. I pray about it.

Not that all those things are good, but here is a list of things that could help you:

1) *Talk about it!* Depression crawls into life as shame and guilt. Just like most other circumstances that we feel guilty about, we tend not to talk about it. But, as C. S. Lewis once put it, "The frequent

attempt to conceal mental pain increases the burden: it is easier to say 'My tooth is aching' than to say 'My heart is broken.' "[viii] Don't just talk about it with people, talk to God about it. Tell God what's on your heart and pray that he will help you. This is good for the mind, body, and soul.

2) *Read through the Psalms.* David walked through depression. Listen to what he says in Psalm 43: "Why, my soul, are you downcast? Why so disturbed within me?" (Psalm 43:5, NIV). Sound like you? One of the side effects of depression is feeling like an island. To hear the heart of David and be able to relate to his depression can help you walk through yours.

3) *Worship.* In those Psalms written by David, he declares that in the middle of the night during depression, God would give him a song to sing, and that it was that song that lifted him out of the night and renewed his spirits.

– "I call to remembrance my song in the night; I meditate within my heart, and my spirit makes diligent search" (Psalm 77:6, NKJV).

– "By day the LORD commands his steadfast love, and at night his song is with me, a prayer to the God of my life" (Psalm 42:8, ESV).

God of the Hills and Valleys

In 855 B.C., Israel's armies and its king marched against the province of Aram. It was fall when the two nations met in the hill country outside of Israel. Though the Israelites were outnumbered ten to one, Aram was defeated.

The king of Aram, Ben Hadad, soon gathered his officials and began to discuss what their next course of action should be:

"We were defeated because they gained the high ground," the officials counseled. "Their god is a god of the hills. But, if we reassemble and grow our army, we will not be defeated."

> God doesn't fall off his thrown when you fall into depression.

"What do you suppose I do then?" the king asked.

"Wait until the spring and attack Israel in the valley. If you do this, victory will certainly come!"

"Alright. We will do as you have said."

Thus, when springtime arrived, the armies of Aram marched against Israel—this time meeting in the prairie land amongst the valley.

Galloping out on horseback, the man of God spoke with Ahab, the king of Israel:

"This is what the LORD says: 'Because the Arameans think the LORD is a god of the hills and not a god of the valleys, I will deliver this vast army into your hands, and you will know that I am the LORD' " (1 Kings 20:28, NIV). And this is what God is telling you and me today.

God is still God in the valley. He doesn't fall off his thrown when you fall into depression. The bottom of the valley is just as much God's dwelling place as the highest mountain.

David says about the bottom, "Though I walk through the valley of the shadow of death, I will fear no evil. For I know that you are with me." (Psalms 23, NIV)

So, when mental illness strikes, worship God.

I love you!

I'm praying for you!

You're not alone!

MW

CHAPTER EIGHT

ROOM OF VULNERABILITY

One of the hardest lines in the sand for me to draw as a youth pastor is concerning *vulnerability*. Many Sunday nights I find myself asking, *"Just how much should I share? Should I share with the youth the reason we can't afford to go on a Summer trip is because the finance committee cut our budget? Or the reason that we aren't staying in houses for Disciple Now is because no one wants seventh-grade boys?"* I even find myself asking questions like *"How much should I share about my personal life? Should I expose some of my temptations? Should I reveal some of my shortcomings?"*

You have probably found yourself asking similar questions:

- Should I tell my kids Daddy left us for another woman?
- Should I tell LJ the reason Santa can't bring many presents this year is because Mommy lost her job?
- Do I tell my wife the reason I'm so stressed is because her mother is moving in with us?

A big one for me lately has been:
- Should I tell the church I'm putting out my resume so that I can afford to get married?

Vulnerability takes wisdom to manage. It doesn't come at a small price; neither for tongue nor soul. Often, these conversations arouse in us the chicken-egg debate about trust and vulnerability.

"How do I know if I can trust somebody enough to be vulnerable?"

"Can I build trust without ever risking vulnerability?"[i]

I think both are true; we must trust enough to be vulnerable and be vulnerable enough to trust. However, a danger lies within using vulnerability for vulnerability's sake.

Brene Brown, a researcher at the University of Houston, gives a magnificent example on the topic:

"A young CEO who was six months into his first round of investment funding came up to me after a talk (on vulnerability) and said, 'I get it! I'm in. I'm drinking the Kool-Aid! I'm gonna get really vulnerable with my people.'

My first thought was, '*Oh, man. Here we go.*' First, when people talk about drinking the Kool-Aid, I get skeptical. It's a pretty terrible reference, and if you have to turn off your critical thinking and chug the groupthink juice to be down with an idea or get on board with a plan, I'm already concerned. Second, if you run up to me excited about becoming more vulnerable, you must not really understand the concept. If, on the other hand, you come up to me and say, 'Okay. I think I get it and I'm going to try to embrace the suck of vulnerability,' I'm pretty sure you understand what's involved.

The conversation started with multiple flags. Not enough for a parade, but close.

I gave him a nervous smile and said, 'Say more.' (another favorite rumble tool) Asking someone to 'say more' often leads to profoundly deeper and more productive rumbling. Context and details matter. Peel the onion. Stephen Covey's sage advice still stands: 'Seek first to understand, then to be understood.'

The excited CEO explained, 'I'm just going to tell the investors and my team the truth: I'm completely in over my head, we're bleeding money, and I have no idea what I'm doing.'

He paused and looked at me. 'What do you think?'

I took his hand and led him to the side of the room, and we sat down. I looked at him and repeated what I had said in the talk, but what he apparently missed: 'What do I think? I think you won't secure any more funding and you're going to scare the people (to death.) *Vulnerability without boundaries is not vulnerability. It might be fear or anxiety. We have to think about why we're sharing and, equally important, with whom. What are their roles? What is our role? Is this sharing productive and appropriate?*'[ii]

Ultimately, in every relationship that deals with vulnerability, there needs to be boundaries that are set and outlined by guiding principles. For example, as a parent, we should ask, "Is sharing this going to teach my kids about money and the importance of living below our means? Or is it just going to get them off my back for a couple of days?"

The Power of People Pleasing

When I was in high school, I shot an eighty-two in the final round of a state golf tournament after holding the lead the previous day. I was so disappointed in myself. After I finished, I went back to the hotel and just cried. *All the effort I put in, all those years of practice, and for what—an eighty-two?*

A few minutes went by until my golf coach eased his way in trying to comfort me:

"Drake, what's wrong man?"

I was trying to gain control of my high-pitched-sobbing voice, but eventually, I said, "Murph, I want to prove to everyone that I'm a good golfer. I want to make people proud. I want to make my Dad proud."

Murphy looked at me and so wisely counseled, "Drake, if that's the case, you're playing golf for all the wrong reasons. It's not about proving to others that you're a good golfer; it's about proving it to yourself. And you know that your dad is and always has been proud of you. So what if you had one bad round? Everybody does."

"Look, Drake. When I first started golf, I couldn't have cared less about what others thought of me—if I could or couldn't play." (To which I mentally deliberated, *yeah because you were always so great.*) "But I wanted to prove to **myself** that I could do it."

That story, extrapolated over golf, may not seem like much—but to me, it really was. Everything from my looks, to sports, to my personality, were all focused on pleasing others. Lecrae says in his book *Unashamed*, "If you live for their (other peoples') acceptance, you'll die by their rejection."[iii] We all want to succeed and excel in life. We want to become successful. The problem arrives when at the core of *what we do and who we are* lies another person's approval.

I saw this in my brother recently. Drew goes to the gym to work out almost every evening. We got to talking about it one day, and I was alarmed when he said, "Yeah, I just want to get into shape so girls will notice me." I laughed at first, but then I thought, *"Is he so different than anyone else?"*

Only a few things are as powerful as approval and acceptance. Truth, for example, is more powerful, I believe, than these two—but not by much. People think it's a long walk from "I'm not enough" to "I'm better than them," but it's actually just a short distance away, standing still, because contrary to what many believe, **both derive from the same place—people-pleasing and self-doubt.**[iv]

When fear creeps its way into our conversations, our emotions begin to leak out self-protection tendencies, and a pattern of thoughts typically follow:

1. I'm not enough.
2. If I'm honest with them about what's happening, they won't think of me the same.
3. No way I am going to be vulnerable about this. No one else does it. Why do I have to put myself out there?[v]

These kinds of thoughts often occur. Like when we confess our sins or when we offer an apology, or when we take a stand for someone being treated wrongly. We often think things like:

1. No one else is telling their sins. And they have tons of issues.
2. De facto, it's their issues and shortcomings that make me act this way.
3. In fact, now that I think about it, I'm actually better than they are.

It takes being secure in who we are as a person and firmly planted in who God says we are to operate outside the forces of acceptance and approval.[vii]

"IF YOU WANT LOVE"-NF

Coming into college, both Catherine and I had previously been in unhealthy relationships. After a few months of getting to know each other, during the weird time between being exclusive to each other and dating (most people call this *talking*, which I think is totally stupid) we were sitting in my car below the tennis courts after practice. We began opening up about our past relationships and just being honest with how hard it had been to trust again. We were willing to give our relationship maximum effort, but letting go entails the possibility of getting hurt, and neither of us wanted to become collateral damage. *I find in these moments, it's better to say how you feel. After all, no one can read minds.*

Secretly, I find it difficult to open up. I have a hard time sharing how I feel, but when she brought up the subject, I was glad she did.

NF, who is my favorite musician, had recently come out with his new album, *Perception*, and on it, had a song called "If You Want Love." (By the way, his latest album, The Search, is fire.) The premise of the song is *if you want to gain someone else's trust, you must trust in return, and if you want to be loved, you must show love.*

I played the song for her, and today it's one of our favorites. I think that moment was a turning point in our relationship. We both said, "I'm willing to be vulnerable if you are."

A few days after that conversation, I mustered up enough courage to ask her to be my girlfriend. She said, "Yes," thankfully. On the downside, we flipped the Mustang a few days later. But somewhere in all the calamity, I remember thinking to myself, "*I love this girl.*" I can't remember the exact date, but it was sometime in late winter as we were out on a lunch date. I jumped in the car, palms sweating and all, and announced my love for her; "Sweetie, I love you." This was the first time I said those words.

A nervous smile was her response. "*Well, this is awkward.*" I got my books from the back seat and headed back to class. "*Yeah, this is what you get. You try to be vulnerable, and you screw up a good thing. You're so stupid.*" The self-doubt started talking, and I regretted ever opening up.

I think we have all found ourselves in a position like that—being upset about opening up. But vulnerability is nothing to be ashamed of.

Anything that takes courage or boldness requires a degree of vulnerability. Think about it. Have you ever done something that required bravery without vulnerability? No, because it is the definition of vulnerability that encompasses the possibility of getting hurt, which in turn, gives way to bravery and courage or fear and anxiety.[viii]

Think about all the people in the Bible who were vulnerable:

- Adam and Eve stood naked before God.
- Abraham rose a knife against his son.
- Stephen was stoned to death in front of everyone. (By rocks not weed.)
- Ruth slept at the feet of Boaz.
- Elijah became depressed and had his depression recorded in the Book of Forever.
- Tamar dressed up at a prostitute just to get Judah to sleep with her.
- Lot offered his two daughters to an angry crowd for the protection of a man he didn't know.
- Noah was seen vulnerable by his sons. (aka, naked)
- Peter repeatedly got shut down by Jesus.
- Isaac was deceived by his youngest boy and his wife.

- Hannah was laughed at for being barren.
- Johnathan knew his father was in the wrong about David.
- Sarah had her husband sleep with another woman so he could have children.
- Joseph cried after seeing his brothers.
- David danced; although he probably wasn't a great dancer.
- Job's friends cried for him because they saw his suffering was too great for words.
- Jesus took on humanity.
- Jeremiah cried a lot.
- Paul lived with everyone knowing his past.
- Onesimus, a slave, had to return to his owner.
- Peter, James, and John got to witness Jesus in the garden during his most vulnerable moment.
- James was the brother of Jesus. Talk about an unfair comparison. I might not consider that vulnerability, but it's at least something.

And we could go on and on naming people who were vulnerable in Scripture. You could fill a page of all the times that you have shown vulnerability. But somewhere along the way, we onboarded the thinking that vulnerability was a bad thing.

A survey was done a few years back to see what people were most afraid of. Public speaking ranked number one, then followed by snakes, spiders, things like that. But what surprised me most about the survey was the number of people who voiced their fear of saying, "I love you" first, and who expressed anxiety while asking their boss for a promotion. What really stopped me in my tracks was the number of men—and women for that matter—who said the most stressful part of their day was asking their spouse to be sexually active.

Brene Brown, who we quoted earlier, has spent her entire life studying vulnerability. After ten years of research in social justice, she concluded that **shame, guilt, self-worth,** and **confidence** were the underpinnings of vulnerability. These two forces: *shame/guilt* and *self-worth/confidence*, were juxtaposed to each other, but were also the emotional control centers of our minds. Whichever you let become the lens by which you view yourself, *shame/guilt* or *self-worth/confidence*, ultimately shapes your identity.[ix]

As I began to unpack this, I realized something; I realized how true that was. See, we either view ourselves as (in) people or (I'm) people.

- (in)effective   (I'm) effective
- (in)sufficient   (I'm) sufficient
- (in)capable   (I'm) capable
- (in)significant   (I'm) significant
- (in)compatible   (I'm) compatible
- (in)cidental   (I'm) no mistake
- (in)efficient   (I'm) efficient
- (in)tolerable   (I'm) tolerable
- (in)secure   (I'm) secure

The difference from (in) and (I'm) may seem small. Perhaps one letter and an apostrophe are the only differences you notice, but that's not so. If you view yourself through success, who you know, what you do, failure, or status, you may find happiness—but only for a short time.

On the contrary, if you view yourself through who God says you are, it will transform your life.

Think about all the things we let define us. Our **circumstances**, for example contend for our identity. Whether we are healthy, rich, divorced, or happy. We let our **positions** speak into our lives. *I am a mom, a dad, a nurse, a student.* I think our **giftings** have a hand in it. *I'm a great _____. I am especially gifted _____.* Our **failures** define us. *I am a recovering _____. My brother is a three-time _____.* **Other people** mold our identity. Whether it's an ex-boss, a co-worker, a friend, a classmate, people are always shouting down their opinions from the cheap seats. Even when people don't speak into our lives, they change our identity. Thomas Cooley said it this way, "I am who I think others think I am."[x] **Social Media** plays a role. To the point that we give others a pen and paper to leave an opinion. The **enemy** leaves a comment. Sad thing is, he has video evidence to back it up. *Remember when you said…Remember when…No way you're strong enough to make it through this.* Most emphatically, **you** define you; even to the extent that we coined the phrase *"I am my own worst enemy."*[xi]

When these identifiers begin to speak out, they create a friction towards worshiping God. However, God is seeking to define and reshape the way you view yourself.

Wet weddings are better than wet wedding rings.

"Did I not weep for those in trouble? Was I not deeply grieved for the needy?" (Job 30:25, NLT)

About seven years ago, our family decided to take a tubing and skiing trip to Lake Sanctuary. After riding around in the boat for a while, Mom decided to jump on the inner tub with our younger sister.

When she announced her plans of jumping off the boat, I told Mom she should take off her jewelry, but did she listen? Nope! "I've been wearing this wedding ring for twenty-years, Drake. It's not coming off now!"

We started the boat, and they rode behind us for perhaps five minutes, until Mom started violently screaming.

I went airborne off the boat. (I literally jumped off the moving boat. Not a smart idea. I don't know what possessed me to do such a thing. Not like I could have done anything, but it was my natural reaction, I guess.)

"Were they impaled by a stick or something?" I'm thinking in mid-flight.

As I was doing my best impersonation of Michael Phelps swimming out to their innertube, Mom was in a full-blooded screaming, crying hysteria thing as I was hollering, "What's wrong? What's wrong?"

When I got about twenty feet out, she finally wailed, "My wedding ring—I lost my wedding ring." I breathed a sigh of relief and swam back to the boat. When I got in, my uncle asked what had happened.

"Ahh, she lost her wedding ring. Should have taken it off like I told her, and this would have never happened."

Laughing, my uncle responded, "That's women for you, Drake. They never listen."

We pulled the boat back around to pick them up, and my mom, who was still scream-crying, explained where it flew off. Sadly, we did not find her ring at the bottom of the lake (talk about a needle in the haystack).

Naively, I thought our searching was over after that evening, but oh no. Mom went full-on detective mode.

Honestly, I didn't know she had this side to her. She called into work and requested the next forty-eight hours off. She had us dispersed all out into the lake with waterproof metal detectors the next day. *Like seriously Mom—where do you even get waterproof metal detectors?*

We spent several hours swimming around searching for the missing ring, but we never could find it.

In actuality, Mom was most nervous about calling Dad. She finally mustered up the courage and told him what had happened. His response was legendary (husbands, take note). My dad, married twenty years, said, "Honey, that's okay. Rings can be replaced—you can't."

Once again, I was stupid enough to think that our searching was done.

The next year, the dam busted, so the lake drained while an engineering team came in and repaired it. Little did I know, Mom had signed all of us up for metal detector duty once again. We were scampering around, digging craters in the ground. We never did find that stupid ring. I still believe my metal detector was defective because my brothers found all kinds of neat things, but all I seemed to dig up was bottle caps. What a bummer!

The point of the story is that women understand crying. Women cry about a thousand percent easier than we men do. (Before you turn me off for sounding anti-emotion or anti-women, that's not what I'm advocating at all.)

When is the last time you heard of a man crying over losing a wedding band? Probably never, because he would be excited over the fact that now he doesn't need to worry about having his finger ripped off during Cross Fit. I once met a guy who had his finger taken smooth off because he went to dunk a basketball. He said it slid off like butter—yuck.

My point is, women get emotion. Look in your worship services. #enoughsaid.

So, we ask the question, "Where are the men?" Somehow, the concept that a man is not supposed to feel has crept its way into our society. Men tend to think:
- My job is to take care of the family.
- My job is to work.
- It is to put food on the table.
- To keep a roof over our heads.
- To own a drivable car.

Not only that, but we have the pressure of knowing:
- There is college to pay for.

- A 401(k) to save for.
- We have the mandate to keep the lights on, the water running, the insurance paid for.
- Don't get me started on the stress of taxes coming around every year.

(Women have these worries also, but right now, I want to address the men.)

Thoughts have crept into the minds of men. We believe being the family caretaker is our primary priority. If we can keep our families provided for, then they should be happy—they should be grateful. But friends, please hear me; that is a colossal lowball.

Your family needs you to be the emotional leader. Your son needs you to be the Godly example. Your daughter needs guidance and direction. Your wife needs to know that she is loved. Sometimes that involves saying, "I love you." Other times, it just involves picking up flowers on your way home from work. Still other times, it means emptying the dishwasher.

See, Satan has tricked us into believing, *if my family is taken care of, then I have done my job*. But that is a lie!

Please do not hear me say that you should be ashamed of working hard or that providing for your family is unimportant. I am not saying that at all. The Bible is clear that a man who does not work does not eat. But what I am saying is that **your family needs a Godly leader**. It's easy to show love in a hateful way as a father and then call it "tough love." Your family needs to know that you care more *for* them than you are burdened *by* them. They need to see you worship, to see you walk after God's heart. Your family needs someone present in their lives. Your wife and kids need to know you love them.

It's not wrong to show emotion. Your family needs not only a provider and a caretaker, but the love of a father who cares for them and the advice from a dad who has *been there, done that*. Sometimes they need a shoulder to cry on or someone to tuck them in. Most of all, your family needs you to teach them about Jesus.

In vs. I'm

For the remainder of this chapter I want to rehash (in) people vs. (I'm) people.

I'm going to share three specific examples of an (in) identity Christian, along with its (I'm) identity Christian counterpart. I want to dig into each of these and discover how to lead, live, and move using Scripture as our guide. *How do we believe in the "I Am" when we know who we are?*

1. (In)different:
Numbing—not facing the emotions you're actually feeling:

"We all numb. We have different numbing agents of choice: food, work, social media, shopping, television, video games, porn, booze (from beer in a brown paper bag to the socially acceptable—but equally dangerous—fine wine hobby) but we all do it.

"Statistically speaking, every person holding this book is affected by addiction. According to the National Council on Alcoholism and Drug Dependence, Inc., seventy percent of the estimated 14.8 million Americans who use illegal drugs are employed, and drug abuse costs employers $81 billion annually. We all find a way to numb the pain. But to what degree?

"Numbing the pain, or taking the edge off, does precisely that. Consequentially, it numbs us of any positive feelings: joy, love, belonging, and other emotions where we find meaning in life," wrote Brene Brown in *Dare to Lead*.[xii]

The almost scary thing in 2020 is that the Church has become a numbing agent—the euphoria of worship.

(I'm)peaceful:
Finding Real Comfort:

Numbing is an attribute of loss of control. Death, shame, pain, stress, etc. are often things that we cannot control. We feel like circumstances are out of our hands, so we numb to cope. But comfort comes when we let go and let God. I know that is cliché, but let me reframe the phrase: comfort comes when peace replaces fear.

Growing up in a small house with parents working full time jobs, I was often put in charge of babysitting my younger brother. One day, I became distracted from babysitting duty by chasing a basketball under our camper. Apparently, my mom and dad were having one of those *get out boys; the grown-ups are talking* conversations.

Well, long story short, my brother ended up at the bottom of the pool. Not old enough to swim, he was drowning. I was only seven at the time, but as soon as I came out from under the camper, the first thing I noticed was Dad in mid-flight jumping into our large

> Comfort comes when peace replaces fear.

green-algae-filled pool in the middle part of December. He grabbed Drew, who luckily had on an orange shirt, and I'll never forget what Drew said seconds after being rescued; "Thank you for saving me, Daddy." It was the most innocent and sweet response.

> Our comfort comes from our Comforter.

Feeling the weight of my brother almost dying, knowing he was my responsibility, I shoved the memory from my mind. But it resurfaced here.

The reason we can find comfort, even in the midst of drowning, is because we have a heavenly father watching over us—even when we don't know it. Our God is sovereign. Sovereign is a pretty big word, but it simply means that our God is in control of everything. Our comfort comes from our Comforter. Our comfort comes from God's power and who we are to him.

2. (In)satible:
"I can't say 'no.'":

Walking the line between selfishness and being selfless can be hard for me. For example, just today, a friend called me and asked for my help setting up his chicken houses. I don't know what to tell him because I hate saying "no." But I also have so much to do; two tests to take tonight, a book report due by the end of the week (and its Wednesday), plus Church to plan for. Every time he has called today, I can't bring myself to pick up the phone. I am so bad at saying what needs to be said; especially when it's the difficult thing to say. But in my profession, as in many others, it is something that must be done.

Maybe you find yourself in a similar situation. *I can't tell my kids 'no,' even when I need to. Every time they ask for something, I ultimately give in. I can't tell my boss 'no.' Every time she wants me to stay late and work, I say 'yes.'* Maybe yours is entirely different. Maybe its food you can't say 'no' to. Or sex. Or Netflix. Or Facebook. Or gossip. Maybe its alcohol, collections, gambling, golf, job opportunities, bargains, vacations, spending money, or wasting time; it could be any number of things you struggle denying. But the inability to say "no" leads into a dark place of much hurt.

(I'm)satiable:
Saying "No":

It seems dodging the two-letter negative actually causes more harm than good.

Don't get me wrong, saying "yes" can often be a great thing, but it is the ability to say "no" that gives your yes power.[xiii]

One of the hardest skills to craft in life is **saying "no" to temptation**. However, that is the outcome of a repentant heart.

It is also difficult to **say "no" to a great opportunity**. *Just because a door is open doesn't mean that God opened it.*

And if God opened it, it doesn't always mean that he wants you to walk through it.

We must also learn to **say, "no" to our thoughts**. I can't tell you how many people I have talked with who struggle with thoughts of depression or suicide or anxiety. And when I ask them if they have ever considered telling their thoughts "no" and "to go away" they always look at me with a confused look. "Well, I don't guess I have ever thought about that before."

Scripture says, "Take every thought captive and make it obedient to Jesus Christ." (2 Corinthians 10:5, NLT). Judah Smith says it this way, "Think about what you think about."

I don't presume we can control every thought that comes into our mind during the picoseconds of life, but I know that we can control the way we manage those thoughts. Whether or not we allow them to have a seat at our table.

3. (In)secure:
Hustling for Your Value:

When people do not know their value or where they fit in, they hustle for it. And not the good kind of hustle, but the kind that is hard to watch; at any moment they could self-destruct. This kind of hustle is difficult to be around. You have probably seen it—maybe within a business partner or fellow competitor or in a grad school student. Nevertheless, it is much less obvious to notice within ourselves.[xiv]

(I'm)secure:
Finding Value from Being Valued by God:

I think Louie Giglio said it best when he said, **"I am not, but I know I am."**[xv]

When I was younger, I lived my entire life trying to become like someone else. In grade school, I wanted to be like Jackson Wall. He had that vibe of popularity. In golf, I wanted to be like Jordan Spieth. I wanted to become the golfer he was; left hand low, talking to your golf ball, Under Armor, everything. This even carried over into ministry. Many nights I stayed up watching sermon after sermon of Louie Giglio. I taught myself to be a good storyteller like him, preach like he did, annunciate like he annunciated.

> It's hard to stop the habits that helped you get to your dreams in the first place.

Most every part of my life was modeled after somebody else. I knew I needed to change and become my own person, but I never did. *It's hard to stop the habits that helped you get to your dreams in the first place.* After all, I was popular like Jackson. I was good at golf. Not as good as Jordan of course, but I was still pretty decent. And people loved hearing me preach and almost always invited me back. But inside, I was empty.

It all led to a conversation with God my sophomore year of college. I knew I needed to become my own person, but when I turned around to 'undo,' I didn't even know who I was. I can't remember exactly how many days passed, but about two days later, I walked into my suitemate's room and found a poster hanging on his wall that, at the top, read, "I AM" and was followed by twenty-four scriptures. I asked him where he got the poster.

"Walmart."

So I got in my car, drove to Wally World, bought the poster, drove back to the dorm, and sat in my room reading the Scriptures over my life.

I talk about this like it's all in past tense, but to be honest, I struggle with it now. I can't tell you how many times throughout writing this book I have had to remind myself, *"Be your own person. Don't try to write like so and so; write like Drake Nelson."*

That being said, here are how those twenty-four verses read. These are just a few places in Scripture where people stepped into their identity and into who they were. Where they saw themselves through the lens of faith and what their God said of them. I believe this is what God is saying about you. This is who you are:

- *I am alive with Christ. (Ephesians 2:6)*
- *I am free from the law of sin and death. (Romans 8:2)*
- *I am far from oppression, and fear does not come near me. (Isaiah 54:14)*

- I am born of God, and the evil one does not touch me. (1 John 5:18)
- I am holy and without blame before Him in love. (Ephesians 1:4; 1 Peter 1:16)
- I am God's child, for I am born again of the incorruptible seed of the Word of God, which lives and abides forever. (1 Peter 1:23)
- I am God's workmanship, created in Christ to do good works. (Ephesians 2:10)
- I am a new creation in Christ. (2 Corinthians 5:17)
- I am a believer, and the light of the Gospel shines in my mind. (2 Corinthians 4:4)
- I am a doer of the Word and blessed in my actions. (James 1:22, 25)
- I am a joint-heir with Christ. (Romans 8:17)
- I am more than a conqueror through Him who loves me. (Romans 8:37)
- I am an overcomer by the blood of the Lamb and the word of my testimony. (Revelation 12:11)
- I am a partaker of His divine nature. (2 Peter 1:34)
- I am an ambassador for Christ. (2 Corinthians 5:20)
- I am part of a chosen generation, a royal priesthood, a holy nation, a purchased people. (1 Peter 2:9)
- I am the righteousness of God in Jesus Christ. (2 Corinthians 5:21)
- I am the light of the world. (Matthew 5:14)
- I am His elect, full of mercy, kindness, humility, and longsuffering. (Romans 8:33; Colossians 3:12)

- *I am forgiven of all my sins and washed in the Blood. (Ephesians 1:7)*
- *I am redeemed from the curse of sin, sickness, and poverty. (Deuteronomy 28:16-64; Galatians 3:13)*
- *I am called of God to be the voice of His praise. (Psalm 66:8; 2 Timothy 1:9)*
- *I am healed by the stripes of Jesus. (Isaiah 53:5; 1 Peter 2:24)*
- *I am raised up with Christ and seated in heavenly places. (Ephesians 2:6; Colossians 2:12)*
- *I am greatly loved by God. (Romans 1:7; Ephesians 2:4; Colossians 3:12; 1 Thessalonians 1:4)*
- *I am strengthened with all might according to His glorious power. (Colossians 1:11)*

MW

CHAPTER NINE

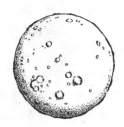

FULL MOON CHRISTIAN

YOU SHINE THE BRIGHTEST IN THE DARK. That is the left hook! Let me say it another way; **in the darkest moments of life, Christ can become the most evident in your life.**

In school, many students ask, "Why am I learning this?" or "When will I ever use this?" It is a shame that the question, for the most part, goes unanswered. Here, I want to show you the finished product—what a full moon Christian will look like. Someone who takes this phrase and lives by it will see the dark times coming, not be afraid, trust God through it, and their faith will grow as a result. Other people will come to know Christ due to their attitude. They will be a blessing to all those who surround them, and the Lord's favor will rest upon them. Do you want to be that person? If so, buckle up!

> You shine the brightest in the dark.

Salty on Sunday Mornings

I grew up going to Sunday school. Honestly, I never had much say in the matter. Like once, when I was younger, Dad and I got a GameCube for Christmas (for those of you who are like, *what is a GameCube?* I am so sorry because your generation missed out on the greatness that was Super Monkey Ball). Dad and I were rascals and thought we could skip out on church, but nuh-uh. Mom came in blaring, "If you two don't get ready, so help me God, you and that game will be in pieces." I would like to say she was joking, but in all honestly, she meant every word.

Even though I went to Sunday school throughout my childhood, I hated it. Not that my teachers were bad, but my heart was. However, during my eleventh-grade year, one Sunday school teacher completely changed my life—Rick Green.

One morning, during Sunday school, I asked Mr. Rick something that we all ask at times: "Have you ever heard God speak to you? Like, is it an audible voice or just a feeling? And how will I know when God is speaking to me?" Wisely, he answered the question with a story.

"Drake, one day, I was driving down the road headed home from work. It had been a long day, and, quite frankly, a long year. As I drove along, I noticed the full moon in the distance. It appeared larger than ever. The color was bright orange, and its light illuminated. I just sat there gazing—admiring its beauty for a while. During that moment, I heard a voice speak to me. I didn't hear it as I did my wife or kids. It was different—indescribable even. The voice said, 'Rick, I want you to be like that moon. I want you to become a *full-moon Christian.*'"

"Hmmmmm," I replied. His answer satisfied my question, but the idea of a full-moon Christian occupied my thoughts.

The next night, as I laid in bed, I kept wondering what Rick meant by full-moon Christian. *Could it be said of me? Was I a full-moon Christian?* Being curious, I spent the next day studying our Moon.

Apparently, we have the fifth largest moon in our solar system. In comparison with the planet it orbits, our Moon ranks #1. The more interesting fact is that moons can't create light. All they can do is reflect the light of the nearest star—in our case, the Sun.

The Moon has eight different phases that happen within a month. The Moon's motion around Earth causes these various stages, and due to its twenty-nine-day orbit, sometimes the Moon reflects ample sunlight and sometimes it reflects only little. But one thing never changes; the Moon is always lit by the sun. Our visibility of it may be limited because we are on Earth, but the Moon is always lit.

While researching the topic, I came across this statement that may shed some light on the subject (get it, shed some light ☺): "Like the Earth, the Moon is a sphere which is always half illuminated by the Sun, but as the Moon orbits the Earth we get to see more or less of the illuminated half."

The Moon without the Sun would be nothing more than a discolored figure that no one knew existed. The Moon doesn't have the capacity to produce light, but instead, it is given the obligation to project the Sun's light to the people of Earth. And for what reason? So that they can see through the night. And the same is true of us.

> We are the operating satellite in a position of reflection.

Now, as for Mr. Rick, his meaning of a full-moon Christian was about becoming someone who was not lukewarm. Here is the astounding truth; Jesus does not want only half of you. He does not want you to become a quarter-moon Christian, and he certainly does not want you to live in darkness. He is calling you and me to throw all our chips on the table and reflect Christ to those around us.

Jesus said, "I am the light of the world" (See John 8:12). But he also called us the light of the world (See Matt. 5:14). Maybe you are like me and wondering, *"Who is it, God? Am I the light or are you the light?"* Both of these can't be true at the same time, can they?

So how do we interpret the teachings of Jesus? Simple: we are the operating satellite in a position of reflection. Jesus is THE light, but we are a mirror.

CLEAR AS DAY

In 2017, we had a total solar eclipse. Some friends and I got together and pitched in a few bucks to order a pair of special eclipse glasses from NASA. When the eclipse began, we all went outside and expected to see a black hole in the sky, but boy were we dumb. Apparently, a solar eclipse takes hours to happen, so we did what typical college students do when they are waiting on the Moon to cover up the Sun—eat. By the time we went to Chick-Fil-A, came back, and put the shades on, the Sun could not be seen. A massive black hole covered the Sun's hiding place. We all went crazy. So crazy, in fact, that people from the neighborhood wanted to borrow our shades to look at the eclipse. (I will say that for the next solar eclipse, you need some of those shades. Without them, it is impossible to see the black hole. It all just seems really bright, but those NASA glasses block out the U.V. rays, and you can see it clear as day. ☺)

Now, was it the Sun's fault that the people on Earth could not see it? Or because it disappeared, did that mean it wasn't there? Of course not. In a solar eclipse, the Moon gets between the Earth and the Sun. In the same way, we can get in the way of people seeing Jesus. When we try to elevate ourselves and make ourselves the center of attention, people do not see Jesus. All they can see is us.

In my life, I have seen some of the nicest people get put into positions of visibility and accept all the worship for themselves. Most every time, God strips them of that position.

There is a story in the Bible of a king who took credit for something God did, and you know what happened to that king? He died. Yep, stone-cold dead. The Bible says, "Instantly, an angel of the Lord struck Herod with a sickness, because he accepted the people's worship instead of giving glory to God. So he was consumed with worms and died" (Acts 12:23, NLT). God takes his glory very seriously. You are walking on thin ice if you try to accept it for yourself.

SUPER BLUE BLOOD MOON

A few weeks after the eclipse, America had its first super blue blood moon in over three hundred years. This happens when a lunar eclipse, a blue moon, and a super moon all happen at once. A super moon means that the moon appears about fourteen percent larger than usual. A blue moon means that it is the second full moon of a month. Additionally, a blood moon means that a lunar eclipse is occurring. There are only two lunar eclipses a year, one blue moon for every two or three years, and only twenty-five percent of moons are super moons. Therefore, the odds of all three landing on the same day are about one in forty-two thousand. They only occur once in every two hundred and sixty-five years.

It was a Wednesday night when this Super Blue Blood Moon occurred, so we had a little viewing party at church with the youth. Just saying, it was scary outside watching a blood moon at church beside our cemetery. #littleboyblue

So, precisely what is a lunar eclipse? **A lunar eclipse happens when the Earth blocks the sunlight from reaching the Moon.** The Earth's shadow gets cast over the Moon so that it appears to be blood red. The Earth gets in the way, and this can be true of our lives as well.

The world can keep you from reflecting Christ. The world will try to tell you how to live, culture will implore you to follow its example, and if you let it, it will stop the SON from shining in and through your life. You need to be *in the world*, yes—making a difference—taking a stand for Christ—reaching the lost—but *not of the world*.

"Star Struck (Text Messages of College Girls)"

Our world has always had its stars, and I don't mean astronomical stars. From the gladiator, to the king, to the artist, to the philosopher, the world has always had people to envy or admire. However, I don't think there has been a time in our history, as is now, where we so want to replicate other people's actions. I have seen this unfold in my own life—watching YouTube videos of other pastors thinking, *If I could only be like them.* I give so much attention to celebrity pastors, and in turn, they have a significant influence on and in my life, even somewhat unknowingly.

I have seen this in my sister lately, who is fourteen. *I know, I know; bless my mom's heart. Three boys and a fourteen-year-old girl. Pray for her.*

So many things go through her mind. What she wears. What she says. What she thinks. What she does. How she does. Why she does. What she aspires to be. What she strives for. Who she is attracted to. Who she dates. Why she dates. All these things, in an extensive manner, come from and are determined by media.

Now, when I talk about media, I am not talking about a Steph Curry, a Leonardo DiCaprio, or some other larger-than-life figure per se, but I am talking about the business side of media that pours thousands upon millions of dollars into investing into the mind of the up-and-coming generation. In our day and age, it is Generation Z. I, too, am of this generation.

The Christians' morals are changing—for the worse I'm afraid. We are watching it unfold. For example, I'm currently taking summer school classes to finish up my graduate degree from New Orleans Baptist Theological Seminary (NOBTS). Today, as I was sitting in class, my teacher said the D-word. The more shocking incident was when my classmates nervously laughed as if he had told a joke. This was no fault on NOBTS. The teacher was just a doctoral intern from (COLLEGE) University teaching a two-week summer class. But as much as I hate to admit it, the sad reality is that his language exemplifies the Church today.

This type of talk has become acceptable.

One of my best friends, who is also a youth pastor, nonchalantly said three or four cuss words at lunch recently.

When I was playing golf with some ministry partners during my undergraduate days, I chipped a ball close for gimme to win the hole, and instead of getting a "Good shot Drake," one of the guys flipped me the bird. He thought it was funny—the bird for a birdie. But I don't need to explain this to you; you already know it. Just look around. Perhaps this is not so in the older generation, but people who consider themselves Christian have no problem with these kinds of actions. Actions like this have become entirely ordinary in the Church today, but why? And has it always been this way?

Plato said this about music, "Let me make the songs of a nation, and I care not who writes its laws." Artists like Lil Wayne, Bruno Mars, Ryan Tedder (OneRepublic), Chance the Rapper, Kendrick Lamar, and Nick Jonas all profess to be Christian while their music would never indicate it. This trend is evident even in Christian music. Andy Mineo, with his new song, "Family Photo," included the D-word. He then defended himself by going to Twitter; "If I say 'Great ******* job!' Out of a joyful heart bc my boy graduated or if I say, 'good job' w[ith] a jealous/hateful heart-which is pure b4 God?"[i] The answer seems pretty simple to me—neither.

Let me sidebar for a moment and share a conversation I read recently from a group text:

Jenifer (RA of a college campus)- "Hey girls. It has

been brought to my attention that I have been offensive lately. If I have offended anyone in any way, I want to apologize."

Shay- "Watcha mean Jen? You haven't offended anyone?"

Jenifer- "Well, I didn't think so either, but apparently, saying the B-word is offensive."

Alexis- "What? People need to grow up. Let's not act like we aren't living in the 21st century. I don't find that offensive at all."

Megan- "F*** yeah. Say whatever you want. You aren't offending us. People don't need to pretend like (COLLEGE) is a Christian campus. People are so sheltered. SMH."

Jenifer- "Well, thank y'all. I agree, but unfortunately, some people in this group chat are still living in the 1940s."

Lisa- "I'm so sorry, Jen. You can say B**** all you want. People are ridiculous."

The conversation went on throughout the night, but many of you have probably found yourselves in a similar discussion. I hate even putting the *'s over where the letters should go. Delivering the idea of a cuss word by *, whatever symbol that is, I am not so sure is not a sin, so forgive me.

Many people have lost the time of silence. Think about it. We run; we listen to music. We drive; we listen to music. We work out; we listen to music. We study; we listen to music. We sleep; we listen to music. We get bored; we listen to music. We work; we listen to music. We shower; we listen to music.

I don't put much stock into studies because you can get a survey to say pretty much anything you want. But in the most recent inquiry done on music, we have learned that Americans spend, on average, thirty-two hours a week listening to music.[ii]

My old youth pastor used to say, "Garbage in, garbage out." When we spend so much time pumping this music into our mind, it is only natural to assume that, eventually, we will reap what we sow. And the results have become evident within the Church.

Netflix has had a similar impact. The normality of sex is taught. Cussing, violence, hate, perversion, drunkenness, and self-pleasure are all exemplified in Netflix. Just the other day, I was watching a Netflix show called Dead to Me, and the most commonly used word started with an F. It's not just Netflix but the entertainment industry as a whole. **It has a way of representing the masses in a way not reflective of the whole. Until eventually, through the power of repetition, the masses have conformed to the industry.** Now I know I probably sound like the grumpy old man bashing this generation in comparison with the Golden Days, but this is what has happened before our very eyes. But where did it start?

To some degree, I think it was gradual. The foundation of it all, I believe, was laid in the systems of higher learning. Absolute truths were done away with, morality was redefined, each person became their own god in the sense that they defined right and wrong, and accountability became invalid because, after all, nothing was wrong in the first place. The average person going through college is taught three fundamentals of life: god is dead; there are no absolute truths with the exception of 'there are no absolute truths,' and morality is relative. Year after year of pumping this teaching into the minds of students laid the foundation of what was yet to come and is now here.

This teaching didn't totally make its way into the Church, but it did have an impact. We taught that God is love, grace supersedes righteousness, and righteousness comes from the interpretation of morality. In turn, this resulted in the modern Christian and it should come of no surprise to me that my teacher said the D-word.

Let's take into account the life of a Christian:

- Twenty hours of watching Netflix per week.
- Thirty-two hours of listening to music.
- Twenty-three years spent in an education system that teaches there is no meaning.
- Looking up to role models who further implement what they see lived out.
- Being surrounded by Christian friends who follow the masses.
- Seventeen hours a week spent on social media comparing lives. Posting whatever gains likes.

Now read this section very carefully. **You are facing some difficult times**. The artists write your music.

Academia educates you. Actors normalize depravity. The athletes serve as role models. The alcohol numbs. The phone rings. The book empowers. And the curb appeal attracts. BUT all this only happens IF YOU KEEP SHOOTING FOR THE WRONG STAR.

There are millions upon billions of dollars being spent each year to make you chase after the wrong star. Somehow, it has become normal to watch pornography. Everybody does it—right? Somehow, within the Church, living together has become okay, cussing has become acceptable, weed has become medicinal, dirty jokes have become funny, hatred has become harbored, and righteousness has become taboo—which is all totally contrary to Scripture. If we want to become full-moon Christians, we must reflect the correct star—the Son. "So how do we do that?" I'm so glad you asked. Let me tell you. It's soooooo simple. Read your Bible and do what it says. That is how you reflect Christ. That is how you reflect the Son.

Therefore, we should do these three basic things:

1) Do our best to reflect Jesus to the world.
2) Do not get in the way of the world seeing the Son of God by taking some of his glory for ourselves.
3) Do not let the world block the SONlight from us.

If we can do these three things, we are well on our way to becoming a FULL-MOON CHRISTIAN.

Midnight in the Bright

Do you remember a few pages ago when I talked about how YOU SHINE THE BRIGHTEST IN THE DARK? I know that these last few pages were a lot to grudge through, but now you have made it to the other side. *Sorry I had to sound all...However that sounded.* The reason I wanted you to know the left hook first was that the finished work is you shining in and through the midnight of your life.

I started this chapter around two o'clock this morning. It is now 6:39 a.m., and I just walked outside to take a break and do you know the first thing I saw? The moon. At the daybreak of dawn, the moon can just be seen. It is white, not really shining. It is not reflecting much sunlight at all, just enough shade to make it visible.

Do you know why?

Because the moon doesn't shine in the day; it shines at night.

The same is true in your life. You may think this sounds like preacher talk and perhaps it is. I like preacher talk. But your best chance to reflect Jesus comes during the midnight hours. Paul teaches us this when he says, "We can rejoice, too, when we run into problems and trials, for we know that they help us develop endurance. And endurance develops strength of character, and character strengthens our confident hope of salvation. And this hope will not lead to disappointment.

For we know how dearly God loves us, because he has given us the Holy Spirit to fill our hearts with his love." (Romans 5:3-5, NLT)

Major League Baseball scouts do not care how great a kid can hit in batting practice. They want to see how well he can hit in a game, when the pressure is added, and everybody is watching.

That is precisely how people view you. Unbelievers are looking at you when you are walking through midnight. They are thinking, "Nowwwwww, that's what I want to see. How does Mr. or Mrs. Christian handle God when their life is falling apart?" But when you stand firm, hold to your faith, and reflect Jesus in the darkness, you can give light to those in need.

Look at what Jesus did. In his darkest moment, he was betrayed, beaten, and carried to a cross. BUT he did not let that stop him from taking the time to minister to the one beside him who needed light. He told the thief on the cross, "Today, you will be with me in paradise" (Luke 23:43, NLT).

When the dark time comes, it is okay to be afraid. Just know that the God you serve is Lord over the midnight. Do not let the initial fright become fear—trust God and use it as an opportunity to show Christ to all those around you.

MW

CHAPTER TEN

ROOM OF RELATIONSHIPS

My father tried out for the Mississippi State baseball team as a walk-on. He didn't make it, of course, but that never deterred him from loving StarkVegas and passing that passion on to me and my two brothers.

As you already know from a few chapters ago, I also love the Golden State Warriors. I started watching basketball during my freshman year of college, and it was almost contagious watching how much fun the Warriors had on court.

Several years ago, Golden State won the 2017-2018 NBA finals, but it didn't look that way for most of the year. The Houston Rockets had a better regular-season record, and the basketball world was waiting to see the two teams face-off in the Western Conference Finals.

After winning two of the first three games, the Warriors were set to play at home on May 22nd. Coincidentally, the MSU Bulldogs were playing against the LSU Tigers that same night. (If there is one team I hate losing to, it's LSU. I would rather get punched in the face.)

Both games were nail biters!

Sadly, both of my teams lost; MSU by a score of five to eight and Golden State by a score of ninety-two to ninety-five. My emotions were shot, and disappointment sank its teeth into reality.

When I say that I take losing hard, I mean that I have a place I walk to beside my pond outside when I get emotionally distraught. I slept there that night! (I know, I know; it's sad.) Thankfully, two weeks later, their chance of redemption came.

The Warriors were set to play the Cavaliers in game four of the NBA finals, while MSU was about to play their first Super Reginal game against Vanderbilt. The Warriors won convincingly, but MSU won due to a walk-off home run by Elijah MacNamee, the "prophet" as I call him.

I went ballistic. I ran around the house jumping with joy and ringing cowbells. I can't even think of words to explain how hype I was! To this day, it is one of my

> What we love has the opportunity to bring us the most joy with success and the most heartache with failure.

greatest sporting memories, but why tell that story? Because in the span of a few weeks, I went from two teams bringing me the most heartbreak, to the same two teams bringing me the most joy, but how? **Because what we love has the opportunity to bring us the most joy with success and the most heartache with failure.** That is exactly how relationships work.

C. S. Lewis said it this way:

"To love at all is to be vulnerable. Love anything, and your heart will be wrung and possibly broken. If you want to make sure of keeping it intact, you must give it to no one, not even an animal. Wrap it carefully round with hobbies and little luxuries; avoid all entanglements. Lock it up safe in the casket or coffin of your selfishness. But in that casket, safe, dark, motionless, airless, it will change. It will not be broken; it will become unbreakable, impenetrable, irredeemable. To love is to be vulnerable."[i]

When a relationship is as it should be, nothing in life compares to it. But when rejection creeps through the back glass, the room of relationships can get messy.

PASSING THE KIDNEY STONE

When I was in the second grade, I began to pee blood. At first, no one knew what was wrong. I went from hospital to hospital to get every kind of test you can think of. One day, because I was so scared of needles and sick of getting my blood drawn, I ran out of the hospital and hid in the parking lot.

Fast forward three months and about twenty different tests, we found out that I had kidney stones all along. They were cutting the tissue on the inside of my bladder causing me to urinate blood. (Yes, I know; gross.) The doctors were going to do a procedure called Lithotripsy to break up the stones but decided that since my bladder was so small and I was so young, it would be best to wait and save surgery as a last resort.

For weeks, I passed kidney stones; some were painless, and some—not so much.

After a few weeks, my urine became clear again. The pain began to subside, and I was cleared to go back to normal life. The crazy thing is, to this day, some fifteen years later, there are several kidney stones from the second grade that still remain. I never flushed them out. Once in a blue moon, I will pass one. Most of the time, pain-free, thank God. But broken relationships work very similarly.

Some are painful, and some are painless. Some take only weeks to heal, and some linger on for quite a while. Some require a specialist to help overcome, and others need only solid advice from a friend. To get hurt by a relationship is life, but the breakthrough comes when understanding comes—the understanding **that life does not hang in the balances of our relationships with people but in our relationship with God.**

Broken Family

If you grew up hating to walk through your front door after school, I am so sorry. A broken family can encompass many different facets of brokenness:

- Maybe your dad was verbally abusive to you and your sister.
- Maybe your parents didn't accept you unless you could perform up to their expectations.
- Maybe your siblings left you out.
- Maybe your mom was a workaholic and never made time for you.
- Maybe you come from a large family and got lost in the crowd of importance.
- Maybe you are living with a stepfamily.
- Maybe you were adopted because your natural family threw you out on the streets.

I don't know what your broken family looks like. Honestly, all families look different, and come with their own unique set of challenges and obstacles to overcome.

Louie Giglio, describing the different styles of fathers at Passion 2019, gave six categories of fatherhood:

1) There is the absent father, either due to death or divorce or disinterest or disillusionment.
2) There is the abusive father story; Yeah, I had a dad present, but I wish he weren't. Abusive

either mentally, physically, sexually, emotionally, or verbally.

3) There is the antagonistic father: the father that wants to compete with you, who never lifts you to new heights. Instead, he drags you down. This father often makes statements like, "I am faster than you. I am better than you." "If you can't do it, I can, and if I can't do it, there is no way you should even think about trying."

4) There is the passive dad: the father who is there, just not making any impact.

5) There is the performance-based dad. You did get the hug—if you jumped through the hoop. You did get the "I love you", but it always came with a conditional clause; "I love you when…."

6) Maybe you were lucky enough to have the empowering dad; the dad who always told you how much he loved you, and not only did he tell you, he showed you. He showed up at the piano recital. He showed up at the tee-ball game. Much more importantly, he showed up when you needed him most. I was lucky enough to have a dad like this. One that I can be proud of. He isn't perfect by any means, but he tries his hardest to be the best father he can be. In fact, I couldn't ask for a better earthly father, but I understand that many people do not walk in this reality. De facto, if you're like most people, your dad probably has some characteristics of all six of these fathers. But not only

do these different forms of fatherhood affect us; different styles of families come knocking on our front door also.

Take for instance the **triune family**. You know, the couple that has only one child. This family has several advantages; less financial stress, less favoritism, and, to some extent, more toys and fewer hand-me-downs. There is not so much fighting for attention (at least this is true for the children; not so much for the parents). However, this family comes with setbacks as well.

Spouses typically struggle to put their marriage first. I think this is due to the love that each shares for their child. To that, I give this advice: *Raising your children is important. It requires you to make sacrifices. But your marriage should never be one of them.*

Next, there is the **tried family**. "We tried so many times to have a child. We tried in-vitro; we've been to every doctor we can afford, but still—nothing." As a result, two symptoms appear; stress and shame. It is important here to note

> Raising your children is important. It requires you to make sacrifices. But your marriage should never be one of them.

the difference between shame and guilt. Many people get these two confused or use them interchangeably, but that shouldn't be.

- Guilt says, "I did something bad."
- Shame says, "I am bad."[ii]

Guilt is often a by-product of a mess-up or mistake, perhaps a sin. But when guilt is allowed to grow, its output is shame. Furthermore, guilt doesn't even have to be present for shame to pull up a seat at the table. And once shame sets in, any sense of self-worth is tossed out the window.

There are the **death and deadweight families**. Though they sound similar, these two are extremely different. The deadweight family contains a family member, or members, who do nothing to contribute—financially, spiritually, or emotionally. They are suckers. They suck all the life from everyone. They suck all the money from the bank, and all the chips from the potato bag.

The death family is as it sounds, a family who has lost a loved one.

In some respect, we all come from a death family because everybody has lost somebody. But what I mean when I say "death family" is a family who has lost an immediate family member—maybe a son or a daughter, a spouse, or a parent—at a young age.

Originally when I wrote, "death family," I thought it sounded too harsh, to personal, to blunt, so I wanted to change it and give it a more friendly name; maybe the faded family or the passed-on family or the lost family. But I decided to stick with the original title. I don't think that there is anything wrong with being blunt. In fact, people going through the grief of death appreciate the realness and the acknowledgment of hurt and pain.

It is never easy dealing with a broken family due to death. To lead your family in that situation is something only the strength of God can help you with. I want to offer two books that could be of assistance. The first one is *Through the Eye's of a Lion*, by Levi Lesko, and the second is *A Grief Observed*, by C.S. Lewis.

There is the **divorced family**: children ping-ponging from one house to another; parents always arguing. Somehow, when a parent sits their child down and says, "Hey... LJ. Look—it's not about you. This is not your fault. This is mommy and daddy's doing. It's our fault." Those words get translated into little LJ's mind as *"It's all my fault. I'm to blame."*

Add to that, the parents' shame and guilt, and the result is devastating.

Divorce can stem from any number of things; abuse, adultery, abandonment, anger, anxiety, finances, fantasies, sexual tensions, opportunity, occupations, death of a parent, differing agendas, differing morals, differing parenting styles; you name it. But no matter how you slice it, divorce is messy.

Maybe you come from the **mixed family**: *Mom moved in with Johnny and his two daughters. Now I'm stuck in the same house with three people whom I barely know.*

From the parent's perspective, they're just trying to love again and doing their best to manage life.

This family is the trickiest of them all because sometimes it can be a blessing but other times, a curse.

There is the **single-parent home**. This family faces an uphill battle and lives on the edge of uncertainty: *"When is Mom getting paid?" "When is Dad coming home?" "Is Mommy going to remarry?"*

From the parent's perspective; *"I am struggling to make ends meet and meet the basic needs of my children. All the while, I'm struggling to keep myself emotionally afloat."*

There is the **adopted family** story; where one or more parts of a family have been adopted and taken in by another. Thoughts of identity tend to spring up in the children, and they try their best to tread the tricky waters of adoption vs. acceptance; acceptance that this adopted family is **MY** family. The parents struggle to walk the fine line between protection vs. allowance: *"I want to protect my child from finding out things that could potentially harm them"* vs. *"I want to allow my children the space needed to become their own person and deal with the reality of their life."*

Lastly, there is the family of four or more whose parents are still together. I call this the **twenty-five-years family**. The main reason for the name is due to the fact that from about the tenth-year anniversary until the twenty-fifth-year anniversary, a family will face more challenges and difficulties than any other time. These challenges will try to draw each family member away from the unit. Typically the parents of the parents begin to get sick and die; the children go through adolescence; money will be tight. The father and son tend to go through the alfa-male phase, causing their relationship to be tense. Any number of hazards can occur within those fifteen years. But if a family can make it through those years, more than likely, it will stay together and endure the test of time.

WHERE DO WE GO FROM HERE?

We all live in and come from one of these nine families. Or if you're like most, you probably have a smorgage board of multiple. Either way, the bottom-line is that families are broken. All families! There are men and women all over the world who dealt with family issues at the age of fourteen, and now, at the age of forty-three, they still find themselves dealing with the exact same hurt and brokenness in their "now" families. But why? Because families are like a self-fulfilling prophecy, repeating themselves through the progression of time. Families encroach expectations, and those expectations turn into realities, and those realities are repeated generation to generation. *But you can break the family tradition.*

> You can break the family tradition.

CHAMPIONSHIP OF A CHAMPION HOTHEAD

When I was a freshman in college, I had a match point overhead that I shanked playing in the state doubles tennis championship. At the time, I wasn't worried because we were up a set and a break, but that commanding lead soon dissipated and we lost. I don't know what happened after the match, but I was livid. I began to smash tennis rackets all over the court. I looked like Gronk spiking footballs except I was spiking two-hundred dollar tennis rackets.

I blanked out mentally.

All I can remember is looking down at the shattered fiberglass everywhere a few minutes after losing the match and seeing my tennis coach walking towards me. *Oh boy, I'm in trouble now.*

Everyone was so shocked because this was totally out of my character, or so they thought. It was such an event that years later walking through Walmart, an older gentleman approached me:

"Hey, are you the guy that smashed the tennis rackets a few years ago at Itawamba?"

"Yep, that was me." Shame and guilt flooded in, but he surprised me when he said, "Dude, that was awesome. You are my hero. I have never seen anything like that before."

I laughed and said, "I'm not proud of it. It took me the whole summer to save up money to buy new rackets."

A few hours after the shanked overhead, dad called me on the phone:

"I heard what happened, Drake. Why did you do that?"

"I don't know. I didn't mean to honestly. I didn't think it through; I just snapped."

"I understand, son. I have a tendency to do the same thing. We have a long line of family history working against us, pointing us to short tempers. But even though we are a bunch of hotheads, you have to learn to control yourself and not lose your temper. I know you don't mean anything by it, and anger is something you will struggle with now until the day you die, but it's never okay to do what you did today."

I knew dad wasn't trying to condemn me, but trying to encourage me to be a better person. A better man.

Even mom who came up after the match shaking her head saying, "You are definitely your father's son," was trying to help me understand the power of genetics.

Through the years, I have found myself battling the same struggles of a previous generation.

People often come up and ask me for my last name. People tend to know us by whom we derive from. I am proud of both my parents and happy to be called their son, but when people ask, "Who are your parents?" why are they asking? Usually, to pass quick judgments on my character, for the better or worse. Though the response to me is typically, "Oh, I love your parents; they are so sweet." Somehow, who I come from determines who I *become*.

I see this in my DNA and my upbringing—my nature and my nurture. The older I grow, the more I begin to act, look, and think like my parents. That is the DNA at work.

If you don't believe that will be true of you, just wait. Let the years go by until you come home from college one Thanksgiving, and Aunt Clancie mentions how much you are beginning to look like your mother. You'll probably smile and play it off like it's not true, but you know it is. For the most part, we will spend our lives battling similar struggles of a former generation.

As for the nurture—the context and culture in which we grow up tend to lean in one of two directions: *I'm never going to raise my kids the way my parents raised me;* or, we take the opposite approach and think, *I'll be lucky if I can be half the mother my mom was to me.* Luckily for me, it was the later. But either way, we are affected by the way we were reared.

> You have the power to flip the script.

So bottom line is this: Life gives you a script. Conception hands you DNA, and then life unfolds accordingly.

DNA has set you on a path. Do not overlook that. Family plays a huge role in life. It has given you a script. But you have the power to **flip the script**. The family you are born into gives you expectations. But **just because you are born into a circumstance doesn't mean that you don't hold the pencil to your**

own story. For me, I had to learn that even though I come from a long line of hotheads, doesn't mean that I have to be one. I constantly have to fight against it, and I believe that's okay. Being a broken person coming from broken people is life. But through the years, I have refused to let a family tradition define the person I am.

Breakups

For some of us, our most somber times have been in breakups. You've done so much in this relationship and opened the door to tremendous vulnerability. You've opened your heart and shared things that are personal to you that most others do not know. You celebrated the birthdays, holidays, anniversaries, and made a plethora of memories together. All of this only to have the relationship fall apart and the guy or girl break up with you. Now you feel empty, alone, sad, and frustrated. Looking carefully and thoroughly to find the one for marriage, but nothing you do seems to work, you end up feeling even further from the altar, exhausted, and lost.

Just like anything else you start in life, you don't begin it with the aspiration to break it off one day. Each of us was created with a longing to be loved, desired, and cherished. We dream of that day we get to say those special words, "*I do.*" Maybe you have already said those words but divorce has crept into your story. We search for love, commitment, affection, and intimacy with one special person. Genesis 2:18 says, "Then the Lord God said, 'It is not good for the man to be alone. I will make a helper who is just right for him.'" If God has made a helper for us, then why is this journey from dating through marriage so difficult?

After a breakup, you fixate on certain thoughts or events. You torment yourself with unanswerable questions such as "What if?" and grief floods in without any warning whatsoever. Even while you're asleep, you find no rest because—there they are—in your dreams.

You can no longer count on yourself to make it through the normal ebbs and flows of life. Destruction of the heart has crept in, and now you're left to paddle back upstream.

To add to the despair, people begin "talking." Rumors flood the avenues and streets of life, and normal, if there is such a thing, has vanished. The problem is that there are no funerals for *normal* life. Nobody really cares that you had a breakup. They don't give you a three-week vacation and bring you dinner every night. Instead, the mundane of life continues on, but not as before.[iii]

In this way, everything that once was a pleasant scene now becomes a thorn in the flesh. A colleague's casual "good morning" feels like a curse. Every happy couple in movies, or in coffee shops, or in songs points out the impossible beauty of love. To add to that, unpleasant surprises such as missing the bus or getting left out of the joke feels unbearable.[iv] Usually, these two are not pleasant, but *a light weight can become unbearable pressure on an already broken soul.*

I am speaking from firsthand knowledge. Although I've had my share of relationships and varying degrees of sadness when they ended, I've had my heart truly broken only once, and it abides in my memory as one of the pivotal events of my life. Although I have happily moved on, I still breathe in the consequences of this incredibly difficult event.

It's easy to question the meaning of life after a breakup—especially the worth of your own. Being a world-class underreactor, I tend to stuff my emotions down and forget that they are even in existence. But gunnysacking comes at a cost, or at least it did for me.

Just to pump the breaks and call a quick time out, maybe even change the subject for a few moments—there is a difference between loving someone and loving the idea of someone. You may certainly fall in love with your conceptualization of LJ, but all the while your sense of who he really is, is completely wrong.

For example, I don't know if any of you are aware of this or not, but there is a phenomenon that tends to pop up in dating relationships called the five-year catastrophe. It means how it sounds, but many times what tends to uncoil is a couple may fake it for years and years, but at some point, an epiphany boils up to the surface where each person realizes the other has changed. Sad thing is, this isn't actually true. What has unfolded is they have fallen in love with someone utterly contradictory to reality. They have fallen in love with their projected selves. This can't go on indefinitely, and at some point, the jig will be up, and all will be revealed as playacting. Everything you romanticized about them is untrue, the blinders are taken off, and the love runs out. "Often—very, very often—heartbreak occurs not because love itself dies, but because our projection onto the other fails, or what is being projected onto us crashes and burns," says Susan Piper in *Wisdom of a Broken Heart*.

Breakups are no fun. In fact, I wonder what it feels like to be God. Just a walk through a relationship where one gives a hundred and ten percent only to have a door slammed shut reshapes everything in the way we view our relationship with God. God has given his heart, and he has said the first, "I love you." He was vulnerable first but think about how many times God has been left on voicemail. God knows all too well the pains of a broken heart, or rejection, or what it feels like to be found unsatisfying.

Maybe there is comfort in that? Maybe not. I don't know. But I do know if you seek a relationship with God first, all these other things will be added to you (See Matt. 6:23).

BREAKUPS: PART II

The best way to deal with the breakup is never to have it in the first place. At least that's true most of the time. I began to think of how to offer relationship advice in a concise, quick fashion when the idea came to mind that I should use proverbs. So this next section is going to be my attempt at that. Here we go!!

(1) Focus on your relationship with God above all else.
(2) Learn from the lazy gardener; the one who doesn't maintain his garden will end up hungry.
(3) Don't allow gunnysacking to creep into your marriage. If you do, it will inevitably fall.

(4) Study is good; being a scholar is better.
Understand your spouse.
(5) Date your mate,
or the Devil will find someone who will.[vi]
(6) Acceptance is like a drug. Once you have it, you
will do almost anything to maintain it.
(7) Control what you can control.
Let go of what need be.
(8) One of the hardest decisions in life to make is
deciding whether to give up or try harder.
(9) Every relationship will not be perfect.
Don't think your marriage is bad
because you had a bad day.
Were you happy every day that you were single?
Then why expect to be happy
every day you're married?
(10) Unmet expectations are as dangerous as a wildfire.
(11) If you find a knife in your back,
change your surroundings.
(12) If you are lonely, don't be alone; make a friend.
(13) Friendship is spelled W O R K.
Marriage is spelled H A R D W O R K.
(14) "Friendship is unnecessary, like philosophy,
like art... It has no survival value; rather, it is one of
those things which give value to survival."[vii]
(15) "Women, don't just dress up for your girlfriends
when you go out. Dress up for your husbands.
Husbands, don't quit working out just because you get
married. Continue to date your mate."[viii]

(16) "Marriage works best when two people
who are head over heels in love with Jesus
wake up one day to God's person for them, and that
person is head over heels in love with Jesus.[ix]"
(17) If you think you are happy,
just wait, you will be miserable soon.
(18) Signing a piece of paper is easy,
forgiveness is hard.
Learning to love again is even harder,
forgetting is impossible.
(19) Time heals all wounds is a lie,
But Jesus does.
(20) Men cannot read minds,
yet women expect it.
Communicate your wants.
(21) Sex is powerful,
Love is more powerful.
(22) As time changes, so do people.
Don't be blind to it; learn to adapt.
Learn to love your spouse again.
(23) A broken record will not fix itself.
(24) An eagle has many abilities.
A person has many roles.
Every relationship encompasses uniqueness.
(25) If your presence doesn't make an impact,
your absence won't make a difference.

Broken Communication

The third wall in the "Room of Relationships" is broken communication. I don't think it is our fault.

We didn't ask for this. We never asked for social media with all of its perceptions of being social only to find out that we were lied to. We never asked for the iPhone. We never asked to be carriers of infinite amounts of information in our pockets. Sure, we may have bought an iPhone, but we weren't there when Steve Jobs launched it. We never asked to be so reliant on technology that we need it to date, or so invested in other peoples' lives that we neglect our own. We weren't ready for all of this. Society wasn't ready. If you give your car keys to a six-year-old, what do you expect to happen?

Take Netflix, for example. It's easy to stay up all night binge-watching, only to wake up the next morning with an hour's worth of sleep. You catch the bus, maybe eat breakfast, then sleep through class. At work, you grudge through the day. You become so spent that you lack the energy it takes to develop relationships. Then what happens? You get home from work or school and take a nap, wake up at eight o'clock feeling somewhat rested, cook dinner, eat, clean, focus on your studies, and then what? It's midnight, but you just woke up four hours ago. You aren't ready to go back to sleep, so you watch more Netflix, and when four or five o'clock hits and you become tired again, you sleep for about an hour or two, only to wake up the next morning and repeat the cycle.

This drains you emotionally and relationally to the point that you don't have the energy to connect with people in a meaningful way. It's not just Netflix; it could be a number of things that keep you up: online shopping, scanning Facebook, porn, sex, work-related stress, school projects, our neighbor's dog, you name it. But it's not just sleep deprivation that drain us relationally; it's also the lack of silence.

This generation, unlike any other, has the ability to banish silence from existence. We can tweak and tune our lives in such a way that we are always taking in information. We are not even talking about the *bad* things. We can fill our lives up with GREAT activities. We can listen to the best podcasts, the latest and greatest Ted-talks, a new series on dating from Ben Stuart, the fire Hillsong album they just released, a sermon podcast from Passion City Church, or an audiobook from Timothy Keller. And so, we can **output quiet**. But this comes at a cost.

The American Psychology Association came out with a recent study that showed when we listen to a podcast or sermon, for instance, our mind can't engage socially. What happens is we get into a social setting after listening to three hours of podcasts, and we zone out. We don't engage socially because we are socially drained. We listen to Carl Lentz for three hours while we are alone, to then walk into a social setting feeling mentally exhausted. And where does this lead? To a breakdown in relationships.[vi]

Just the other day, Brandon, one of my best friends, and I were shooting skeets with his kiddos, when he asked a typical question I get, "Hey buddy, you okay?"

"Yes, why do you ask?"

"I don't know; just seemed like something was bothering you buddy?"

My very casual response, "Nah, I'm okay."

But my mind was not so casual. I hated his question. *Is there really something that wrong with me? Do I act upset or disengaged even when I'm not?*

In actuality, what happens is I spend so much time cooped up inside working on this book or sermons or school that it becomes difficult to switch from deep thought to being social.

A few shots later, I asked Brandon how I seemed upset.

"I don't know buddy, just quiet, not as talkative as you normally are."

"Ahh. Honestly, Catherine tells me the same thing. I think it's because I have been stored away in the house writing all morning. When I get in a writing zone, it's hard for me to come out."

Because I know this to be true, I try extra hard to make small talk even when it's difficult, and my mind wants to wonder.

And in this same way, when I am two hours into a YouTube vista or four episodes into my favorite Netflix series, it becomes difficult to make friendships and have meaningful connections with people three hours later when I'm at family dinner.

I don't want to only point out a problem without offering a solution as well. I live life by this rule. Whenever a problem comes up or a complaint arises in the church, instead of gossiping about how bad things are, I make it my goal to create a solution before complaining. I don't want to be known as a problem locator but a problem solver. Here are three practical steps to help with this dilemma:

Step #1: **Engage in small groups**—What we have decided to do as a church to combat this social norm, is develop small group opportunities so that individuals can connect and create those friendships. Sunday evenings at five o'clock we grab dinner, break up into groups of three to five people, and talk about life.

Relationships play an essential role. They give us meaning and make life worth living. It is important to plug into a small group so that if the worst happens and the bottom falls out, you will have a support group to catch you.

Step #2: **Tell people, "hey."** — A study was done a few years back that said a person needs seven acknowledgments a day to feel seen. When this study first came out, I was in high school, so I made it my mission every day to acknowledge at least seven people and tell them "Hello." It was wonderful to see the impact that this had on others and also myself. From becoming more social,

I met more friends, and I also felt the joy of developing relationships. Telling people "hey" was good for my soul.

Step #3: **Unplug from technology**. — The average adult consumes five times more information every day than their counterpart fifty years ago. Further, we spend as much as eleven hours a day in front of TVs and computers—and that's while at home![x] Take a sabbath from your phone. Pick any day of the week to set your phone aside and spend time with people you love.

Step #4: **Teach people how to treat you**. —"You teach people how to treat you by what you allow, what you stop, and what you reinforce." – Tony Gaskins

Step #5: **Be yourself**. — I'll never forget the conversation I had with a young man named Joey Smith. Joey is a unique person and comes to youth on Wednesday nights. I guess you would just have to know him to understand, but he is one of the nicest people I know. One day he walked in the youth room with a different facial expression than I had ever seen. I smiled and said, "Hey Joey," hoping to brighten his day. I knew something was up, but I didn't want to embarrass him in front of everyone, so after the service, I approached him and asked what was on his plate.

"Well, everyone keeps telling me who I should become. Like, I know I'm different, Drake. I know that I am not like the typical guy, but honestly, I don't want to be. I like the person I am, and I'm not going to change for anyone—my mom, my sister, my girlfriend, no one."

I respected Joey so much more after that conversation. He was confident enough to say, "This is me; like me or don't. I am who I am." He inspired me to become a better person that night because I am always worried about what other people think of me. **I want people to like me, but more importantly, I am coming to understand, is the fact that people like me for me and not for who I portray myself to be.**

A Note on Blaming God

I think it is important to sidetrack for a moment and bring some theology into light. That may seem like a big word, but simply put, *theology is the way we view God*. When someone hurts us, we tend to look at God as if he is to blame. "God, why did you allow my wife to cheat?" "God, why did you allow my boss to throw himself at me publicly? I am so embarrassed." Though it may be easy to shake our fists at Heaven, instead of at the one who hurt us, it is important to know that God cannot control someone's actions and still call them free. Since humanity has the capacity to sin or not sin, don't blame God for someone else's sin.

Broken Trust

Trust is like a river: once it changes course, there is no going back to how it was. Promises tend to break like an egg on hot pavement.

When I was younger, I entered into a relationship where, little by little, trust began to fade, on my side and hers. After four years of dating, we turned around to fix the brokenness only to find it was unfixable. The only fix was to forget, which would only lead to more brokenness, so we had to separate.

I have heard it said many times: "Trust takes a lifetime to build but only a minute to lose." Though I agree in part, a question that undermines such a statement is, "How is trust built?"

A researcher in mental health, speaking on that same topic, gave this story that I think will help us here now:

"When my daughter, Ellen, was in third grade, she came home from school one day, closed the door behind her, looked at me, and then literally slid down the front door, buried her face in her hands, and started sobbing.

My response, of course, was, 'Oh, my goodness, Ellen, are you okay? What happened?'

'Something really embarrassing happened at school today, and I shared it with my friends, and they promised not to tell anyone, but by the time we got back to class, everyone in my whole class knew.'

I could feel the slow rising of my internal Mama Bear. Ellen told me that it had been so bad that Ms. Baucum, her third-grade teacher, took half of the marbles out of the marble jar. In her classroom, there is a big jar for marbles—when the class collectively makes good decisions, they get to put marbles into the jar; when the class collectively makes bad decisions, marbles come out. Ms. Baucum took marbles out because everyone was laughing, apparently at Ellen. I told my daughter how sorry I was, and then she looked at me and said: 'I will never trust anyone again in my life.'

My heart was breaking with her. My first thought was, *'(That's right) —you trust your mama, and that's it. And when you go to college, I'm going to get a little apartment right next to the dorm, and you can come and talk to me.'* An appealing idea at the time. But instead, I put my fears and anger aside and started trying to figure out how to talk to her about trust and connection. As I was searching for the right way to translate my own experiences of trust, and what I was learning about trust from the research, I thought, *'Ah, the marble jar. Perfect.'*

I told Ellen, 'We trust the people who have earned marbles over time in our life. Whenever someone supports you, or is kind to you, or sticks up for you, or honors what you share with them as private, you put marbles in the jar. When people are mean, or disrespectful, or share your secrets, marbles come out. We look for the people who, over time, put marbles in, and in, and in, until you look up one day and they're holding a full jar. Those are the folks you can tell your secrets to. Those are the folks you trust with information that's important to you.'

And then I asked her if she had a friend with a full marble jar. 'Yes, I've got marble jar friends. Hanna and Lorna are my marble jar friends.' And I asked her to tell me how they earn marbles. I was really curious, and I expected her to recount dramatic stories of the girls doing heroic things for her. Instead, she said something that shocked me even more. 'Well, I was at the soccer game last weekend, and Hanna looked up and told me that she saw Oma and Opa.' Oma and Opa are my mom and stepdad.

I pushed Ellen for more details. 'Then what?'

'No that's it. I gave her a marble.'

'Why?'

'Well, not everyone has eight grandparents.' My parents are divorced and remarried, and Steve's parents are divorced and remarried. 'I think it's really cool that Hanna remembers all of their names.'

She continued, 'Well, Lorna is also my marble jar friend because she will do the half-butt sit with me.'

My very understandable response: 'Lord have mercy, what is that?'

'If I come in too late to the cafeteria and all the tables are full, she'll scoot over and just take half the seat and give me the other half of the seat so I can sit at the friends table.' I had to agree with her that a half-butt sit was really great, and certainly deserving of a marble. Perking up, she asked me if I have marble jar friends and how they earn their marbles.

'Well, I think it might be different for grown-ups.' But then I thought back to the soccer game that Ellen was referring to. When my parents arrived, my friend Eileen had walked up and said, 'Hey, David and Deanne, it's great to see you.' And I remembered feeling how much it meant to me that Eileen had remembered their names.

I tell you this story because I had always assumed that trust is earned in big moments and through really grand gestures, not the more simple things like a friend remembering small details in your life. Later that night, I called the doctoral students on my team, and we spent five days going through all the research around trust. We started looking into trust-earning behaviors, which enforced what Ellen had taught me after school that day. It turns out that trust is in fact earned in the smallest of moments. It is earned not through heroic deeds, or even highly visible actions, but through paying attention, listening, and gestures of genuine care and connection."[xi]

TRUST ISSUES

After I tore my ACL, it was hard for me to be the athlete I was before. With every cut came the fear that my knee would crumble and with every landing arose insecurity. Why was this? Because I lost trust in something that had always been there. When it left, I was broken, and it affected the way I played sports. The same is true with our trust in people. **When it is broken, it's not that we do not want to trust again, it's that we cannot. We lack the ability to forget what happened; even though we may have forgiven.**

Trust can't just appear out of thin air, no matter how bad you want it to. Trust is unlike forgiveness. Forgiveness is optional, you can choose to forgive or not—but trust is different. *Trust isn't a choice, but a reality of the relationship at hand.* Trust is built, and built, and built, until one day, someone, perhaps even unknowingly to us, has earned our trust. But once that trust is broken, the jar of marbles cannot magically be full again; it takes time. Sometimes small holes form in the bottom and cause marbles to leak out over time. With every three marbles entered, two come out.

Perhaps you are thinking, *"I can show someone trust anytime I want."* That is true, but actions of trust can be given without actually trusting

Don't overlook the left hook: **We are not called to trust people again who have hurt us. Many times, that is impossible. But we are called to give them the opportunity to earn back their trust.** Take, for example, Joseph.

If you think you deal with trust issues, look at what he had to deal with. First of all, his father didn't trust in his dreams: trust issue #1. This kid's family threw him in jail: trust issues #2,3, and 4. Then his master's wife lied on him: trust issue #5. Potiphar threw him in jail: trust issue #6. The cupbearer forgot about him: trust issue #7. After he forgave his family, they still thought he was going to have them killed: trust issue #8. And we could go on and on with this guy's trust problems, but time and time again he didn't make trust appear from thin air because that would have been impossible. But he gave others the opportunity to earn back his trust. His final synopsis of every broken relationship he endured is probably the most powerful verse in the Old Testament; "You intended to harm me, but God intended it all for good." (Genesis 50:20, NLT)

He didn't lie about it; he was real when it came to his relationships. "Yep, you guys are crappy brothers; meant it for evil. Yep, Potiphar's wife lied about me, meant it for evil. Yep, cupbearer forgot me; he is just ignorant." But through it all, God had bigger plans for Joseph, and he has bigger plans for you and me.

The most important thing to Joseph was not his relationship with other people, but his relationship with God. When his brothers sold him, God restored him. When Potiphar threw him in jail, God was there with him. When he was forgotten about, God noticed him. His relationship with God sustained him through every broken relationship, and the same is true in your life. Anyone can hold the helm when the waters are calm. But when the storm comes, jump out of the boat and walk to Jesus.

When your husband cheats on you, your best friend lies to you, your sister walks out on the family, or your boss fires you, worship God. It is that relationship that WILL sustain you through every breakup, broken family, broken conversation, and broken heart incapable of trust.

MW

CHAPTER ELEVEN

NOONDAY AND SUNBURNT

"You want any sunscreen?" Catherine asked as we were walking out of the condo, heading to the beach.

"No thank you, Mom," I replied smiling.

Punching my shoulder, Catherine replied, "I am not your mom."

"Well, you asked for it. I mean look at me—I'm half Mexican. I don't burn."

Catherine's sister, Elizabeth, chimed in, "When I beat you in golf tomorrow, I don't want you using 'I'm sunburnt' as an excuse!"

Elizabeth is an amazing golfer and coaches for Auburn. She could probably beat me blindfolded on one leg. But I would never admit that to her.

I am pretty laissez-faire when it comes to using sunscreen, so I smiled, looked back, and replied, "I'll be fine. Thank you, though."

Catherine comes from a pale-skinned family, so

when I tell you they use a lot of sunscreen, believe me—it's excessive. On a three-day beach trip, they used upwards of fifty bottles. No joke. Fifty bottles. When we arrived at the water, everyone within seventy yards started coughing up wind-blown sunscreen.

Her mom double-checked with me one last time before using the last bit of sunscreen for herself; "You sure you don't need any? At least on your shoulders?"

"No ma'am, I'm okay." In all actuality, I would have probably taken some, but after all the cheap shots directed towards Catherine's sunscreen obsession, there was no way I could save face if I gave in.

I grabbed a towel, laid it on the sand, turned on Pandora, and there I sat. Occasionally, I would get up to throw football or cool off in the water, (mostly a disguise to pee) but for the majority of the day, I baked in the sun.

Going to the beach for that long is boring to me. Once I build a sandcastle, get a tan, and boogie board for about fifteen minutes, I'm ready to go do something else. But since I was with her family, I decided to stay out—**FOR THE NEXT EIGHT HOURS!**

Around five o'clock that evening, Catherine, Elizabeth, and I packed up our things, washed our feet, and eased back towards the condo.

"Umm, Drake, are you okay?" Catherine asked.

"Yes? Why even ask such a question?" I retorted

"Because you're red."

"Oh yeah, you're definitely red, Drake," Elizabeth said laughing. She offered to take a picture to show me, but judging by the looks on their faces, I didn't want to know.

"Nah, don't worry about it. I'll look in the mirror when I get in the bathroom."

It didn't take long for the shower to inform me just how ballistically burnt I was.

"Owwwwwww, hotttttttttttt," I yelled running out of the bathroom. I knew then that my arrogance of not putting on sunscreen was going to cost me. What I didn't realize in that moment was how much.

I had experienced second-degree burns and spent the next two days lying in bed with water blisters from my legs to my shoulders. For the rest of the vacation, I would have to be doused in aloe gel and a weird concoction of olive oil and vitamin E oil every few hours just to ease the pain.

When I finally got home, I didn't sleep for weeks. I couldn't. Every time I rolled over it felt like an electric shock sliding down my shoulders.

Looking back, the scariest part was not knowing that I was sunburnt until it was too late. I didn't feel the symptoms of being burnt during the day until I jumped in the shower that evening. And those few hours spent in the heat with no sunscreen caused for many long sleepless nights full of pain. And so it goes for us.

Our midnights are a mirror.

It is easy to walk down the wrong path, forget all about God, and become totally oblivious to the pain that it's causing or the damage it's doing in our lives—that is…*until we face the midnight*. Our midnights are a mirror which show us the reality of our time spent in the cool of day.

Levi Lesko says it this way, "Train for the trial you're not yet in."[i] To adapt that counsel into our discourse today, *Build a shelter in the calm, so that when the storm hits, you will find safety.*

One of the struggles I've found through writing this book has been language. *How do I take these mental impressions and communicate them in a way that makes sense? Moreover, how do I organize them so that the reader can receive revelation as they are drawn in with a desire to keep reading?* It's hard to assemble such a thing, but since clearer is always kinder, I want to talk about three individuals who spent their time in the calm preparing for the calamity.

Noah

Whenever you think of Noah, what's the first thought that comes to mind? Probably Noah's ark, right?

We typically think of Noah going through storms and deep waters. But before the winds came, I want to turn our attention to some habits that prepared Noah for the flood.

You most likely know the story of Noah's ark. You probably learned it as a kid watching VeggieTales or going to Vacation Bible School, so I am not going to rehash it. I don't really have the page space nor the time. But we can infer that each morning when Noah woke up, he never had to ask, "What am I doing today?" He already knew. "I'm doing the same thing today that I did yesterday, and the day before that, and the day before that, and the day before that—I am building an ark."

Now I used to work in a lumber yard, so I envision Noah walking up to the front desk of Home Depot and saying, "I need about forty-five million 2'x4's, eleven million 4'x4's, fifty million 2'x16's. I need three billion screws, three drills, a hundred-and-sixty-eight million nails, a hammer, and fourteen screwdrivers. I need a skill saw, three blades, a leveler, a sander, ten-thousand feet of extension cord. And oh yeah, I also need about forty tons of tar. Got all that? Just put it on my account. I'll repay it after this flood."

I have always imagined the eighteen-wheelers backing up into Noah's yard dispatching the lumber. *But that's not how this works—that's not how any of this works.* (I hope you got that reference. ☺)

Noah had to find the trees, cut the trees, drag the trees, design the boat, make it waterproof. Noah had to find a way to make the boat three stories tall, build a holding tank to store the animals, and solve the puzzle of how to feed all those assorted creatures.

Noah was by himself. At most, he had the help of his three sons. He did not have power tools, eighteen-wheelers, an engineering team, electricity—nothing.

A replica of the ark was fabricated in Kentucky during 2016. Just to cut down the trees alone, Colorado Timberframe employees worked twenty-four hours a day, seven days a week, for eleven months, to gather the one-hundred-and-eight semi-truckloads of wood to build the ark. The replica itself weighed over four million pounds and cost ninety-one million dollars to erect.

Overall, the project took eighteen months to complete and involved a thousand workers.[ii] If erecting a non-floating replica which wasn't waterproof and couldn't house thousands of animals took that much effort in 2016, consider Noah. He had to be the most physically fit human ever.

Who knows what tools he had? Probably something equivalent to an arrowhead and a butter knife. Nevertheless, Noah had a job to do because it took work to create something that would protect him through the flood.

Not only that, but I imagine people would randomly drop by Noah's tent: "What are you doing here?" Noah would ask.

"Oh, we were just wondering if you were okay," his critics would say, "like mentally. Because this is the dumbest idea ever. Like, what is rain? Water falling from the sky? This is so stupid. Not to mention you're wasting all the wood we need to build houses."

"Well gentlemen, laugh if you want, but when you all get swept away, and I am singing *Row Row Row Your Boat* in my ark, you will wish you would have listened to me."

> Noah built in the calm to prepare for calamity.

Noah built in the calm to prepare for calamity.

The ark did not produce itself.

No.

Noah gave up a former way of life in order to prepare for the flood. In other words, Netflix and chilling will not build you an ark. Scrolling through Instagram—not gonna build you an ark. The average person spends eleven hours a day in front of a screen.[iii] If you want to build an ark, you are going to have to put down the phone and grab the hammer.

WORDS OF WISDOM FROM DAD

When I was in the sixth grade, I began to learn to play tennis. I had moved into a house that had a tennis court in the back yard. Although the court reminded me of the one from *Airbud* (the original, not the pathetic excuse for a sequel), it was good enough to hit tennis balls on.

The first three months of learning to play were the most difficult. I wanted to play by just tapping it over the net, but Dad insisted that I learn to play the right way.

My dad would always say, "Low to high, Drake. Roll your wrist. Move your feet, son." I was furious. I just wanted to poke the ball in and play with my friends. But nope. After practicing for hours one day, I went to my room and began to just sob uncontrollably. I don't know why or for what, but I just cried. Dad came in, and—knowing he needed to address the situation tenderly but with wisdom—taught me a lesson that I will never forget:

"Drake, people always say, 'practice makes perfect,' but that's not true. Although practice will make you more of what you already are, it's not practice that makes you perfect—it is practicing perfect that makes you perfect. You can sit here for hours and just get the ball in but never be any good. Or you can learn the correct way to swing, and you can be good at tennis for the rest of your life."

After that talk, I was determined. I practiced every day that summer until I eventually learned to play the correct way. My sophomore year of college, I won the Mississippi Junior College State Championship and played my next two years at Mississippi College, but I cannot take credit for any of it. It was my dad who taught me how to play and the importance of making good habits all those years before.

My dad can teach anybody how to do anything. It is definitely one of his gifts. But the unexpected lesson did not just stick with me in tennis. It also carried over into other aspects of life. Creating habits is of little to no avail **unless we are creating the correct ones**.

When I was in the sixth grade, it was important for me to get in the routine of reading my Bible. To make anything a habit, it is said you need to do it for thirty days. So, I read my Bible for thirty days straight—only reading small passages of Scripture.

Malcolm Gladwell wrote this about habit making; "To become an expert in any field— sports, chess, neurosurgery—you must practice for ten thousand hours, which is roughly four hours a day over the course of ten years."[iv] I think Gladwell was on to something; if you want to become great, it's spelled W-O-R-K.

Andre Agassi, in his biography, talks about his experience growing up playing tennis. His dad would force him to hit tennis balls for hours every day. Practicing hour after hour, for twenty years, Agassi eventually won Wimbledon.

Years later, in his book, *Open,* Agassi wrote, "If I've learned nothing else, it's that time plus practice equal achievement."[v]

See, habits make a routine, a routine makes a lifestyle, and a lifestyle makes a personality. And you are your personality. Let me repeat that to help it sink in: habits make a routine, a routine makes a lifestyle, and a lifestyle makes a personality. And you are your personality. So, if you want to change, change your habits.

> **Belief only drives actions to the degree of importance that your belief carries.**

We have this Freudian presupposition to where we think we must get to the root of our problems in order for our actions to change. That's not true at all. I'm not saying that as Christians we shouldn't try to clean the inside of the cup—but sometimes we aren't going to find improvement by identifying the root of our issue. **Belief only drives actions to the degree of importance that your belief carries.** Instead, let's put some better habits into place.

Get into the routine of going to church. That's a great thing. I have heard several preachers say we shouldn't make a habit out of going to church, but that couldn't be further from the truth. I understand what preachers mean when they say that—*don't lose the awe of coming before God*. But going to church is an important habit to have. Being a part of the Body of Christ is awesome. Just cultivate and keep the awe factor in it.

EATING HOT POCKETS

A boy in our youth group, coincidentally named Noah, is about six-three, two-hundred and fifty-five pounds. Not to mention, he is only twelve years old. He is a beast. He is the only guy I have ever met to grow a full beard by age twelve.

One day, I brought cupcakes to church. I had plenty, so I told the youth to get as many as they wanted. I assumed there would be no logical way the youth group could eat all those cupcakes. But Noah ate, and ate, and ate. And fourteen cupcakes later, he was full, and I had no more cupcakes.

"How did you eat that many? Like for real—where do they all go?" I asked him. "You just ate fourteen cupcakes. I didn't think that was humanly possible!"

His reply amazed me. "Drake, I didn't get this big from eating a Hot Pocket. I eat a lot." And the same is true in our lives. If we want to grow in our faith and become the person that God wants us to become, it is going to require action—the work of creating the right habits in our life so that every day we are growing into who Christ wants us to be.

MW

The ~~Eight~~ Seven Habits of Christianity

#1) *Live life as you wish you would have five minutes after you die*. Five minutes after you pass, everything will be put into a new perspective. Your house won't be on your priority list. The car you drive will not matter. As much as it pains me to say, the Warriors losing the 2018-2019 NBA Finals won't make a difference either. The only thing that will matter is what you and I have done for Jesus.

#2) *Pray*. Talk to God. Take the example of Jesus. He did not pray only during the trial, temptation, or testing, but also beforehand. In the Lord's Prayer, he prays, "Lead us not into temptation, but deliver us from the evil one." (Matthew 6:13, NIV) Pray alone. Go somewhere that you can talk out loud. Pray for the impossible. Have faith that God will come through. Pray as Jesus prayed, "Lord, take this cup from me, but may your will be done."

#3) *Read your Bible*. It is near impossible, if not completely impossible, to become everything Christ wants you to become if you don't spend time in his Word. Ravi Zacharias says it like this, "If you want to gain wisdom, get in the Scriptures and around someone who has been through a lot, yet their faith was not shaken."[vi] Reading your Bible can be compared to a single mom who gets an envelope. In the envelope, there is a signed blank check. The family is living below the poverty line and seldom gets to eat three meals a day. She becomes busy and places the envelope on her bedside table collecting dust, but she never takes the time to open it—though what is inside could solve many of her problems and prayers. In the same way, the Bible, if left collecting dust unopened beside our bed, will never do us much good. It is only by opening it that we discover its beauty and treasure.

#4) <u>Be strong and courageous</u>. Do not be afraid of what God has planned for you in the future. Embrace it and move forward in faith.

#5) <u>Obey the teachings of Jesus</u>. The Bible is clear about this point. Let's take a look into Scripture:

> *As Jesus was starting out on his way to Jerusalem, a man came running up to him, knelt down, and asked, "Good Teacher, what must I do to inherit eternal life?" "Why do you call me good?" Jesus asked. "Only God is truly good. But to answer your question, you know the commandments: 'You must not murder. You must not commit adultery. You must not steal. You must not testify falsely. You must not cheat anyone. Honor your father and mother.'"* (Mark 10:17-19, NLT)

Though the law must be held, how do we define it? On to #6!!

#6) <u>Love God and Love People</u>. Jesus says, "All the Law and Prophets hang on these two commandments; love

God and love People." (Matt. 22:4, NLT) Most, if not every, question in your life can be answered correctly if you obey these two commandments.
- "Lord, is it a sin to drink?"
- "Lord, how far is too far if we aren't married?"
- "Lord, is speeding a sin?"
- "Lord, where should I work, or where should I go to school?"

#7) <u>*Do your job*</u>. You have been given a mission from Jesus; *spread the Gospel to all nations*. Fulfill that mission. If you are called to the mission field—go. If you are urged to work at the Polo Outlet Mall—go. No matter where you are in life, wear the name of Jesus there.

Daniel

(What I feel like God is telling me:) *I WANT PEOPLE TO PRAY TO ME IN NOONDAY JUST AS THEY DO IN MIDNIGHT. I WANT PEOPLE TO ACKNOWLEDGE ME WHEN LIFE IS GOOD, JUST AS THEY DO WHEN THE BOTTOM FALLS OUT. THE SPARE TIRE IS ONLY GOOD WHEN ONE GOES FLAT, BUT I WANT TO BE THE VEHICLE BY WHICH MEN GET THROUGH LIFE.*

Daniel was a good-looking young man. He was someone who was well-versed in every branch of learning. He was strong, healthy, knowledgeable, and had all the requirements that the king was looking for to serve in his royal court. **Though Daniel was the guy that everyone wanted to be, he was a man of prayer.**

Daniel had been taken out of his homeland, Israel, and sent to Babylon to serve under three kings: King Nebuchadnezzar, which we will call King Neb for the remainder of this chapter; King Belshazzar; and Darius the Mede who placed Daniel and two others as high officers over the land. The other two officers were jealous of Daniel, so they were going to attempt to have him killed.

They went to the king and convinced him to outlaw prayer—and this is where we pick up in the story:

(10) But when Daniel learned that the law had been signed, he went home and knelt down as usual in his upstairs room, with its windows open toward Jerusalem. He prayed three times a day, just as he had always done, giving thanks

to his God. (11) Then the officials went together to Daniel's house and found him praying and asking for God's help. (12) So they went straight to the king and reminded him about his law. "Did you not sign a law that for the next thirty days any person who prays to anyone, divine or human—except to you, Your Majesty—will be thrown into the den of lions?"

"Yes," the king replied, "that decision stands; it is an official law of the Medes and Persians that cannot be revoked."

(13) Then they told the king, "That man Daniel, one of the captives from Judah, is ignoring you and your law. He still prays to his God three times a day."

(Skip two verses.)

(16) So at last the king gave orders for Daniel to be arrested and thrown into the den of lions. The king said to him, "May your God, whom you serve so faithfully, rescue you."

(17) A stone was brought and placed over the mouth of the den. The king sealed the stone with his own royal seal and the seals of his nobles, so that no one could rescue Daniel. (18) Then the king returned to his palace and spent the night fasting. He refused his usual entertainment and couldn't sleep at all that night.

(19) Very early the next morning, the king got up and hurried out to the lions' den. (20) When he got there, he called out in anguish, "Daniel, servant of the living God! Was your God, whom you serve so faithfully, able to rescue you from the lions?"

(21) Daniel answered, "Long live the king! (22) My God sent his angel to shut the lions' mouths so that they would not hurt me, for I have been found innocent in his sight.

Daniel's prayer in his den at noon prepared him for the lion's den at night.

And I have not wronged you, Your Majesty."

(23) The king was overjoyed and ordered that Daniel be lifted from the den. Not a scratch was found on him, for he had trusted in his God. (Daniel 6:1-23, NLT)

There are so many things that can be said about the story of Daniel, and perhaps you have heard sermons or even read books on them all. However, the number one statement that jumps off the page for me is DANIEL'S PRAYER IN HIS DEN AT NOON PREPARED HIM FOR THE LIONS' DEN AT NIGHT.

MW

Job

The last of the three men I want to speak about is Job. Now you may think it is odd to talk about Job in a chapter called *Noonday and Sunburnt* considering most of the book of Job talks about his suffering.

Before I wrote this chapter, I read the book of Job a few times and highlighted every verse that talked about Job's life before the suffering began. There are nineteen different references towards his former life. (Job 1:1, 1:5, 1:8, 1:21, 2:3, 2:10, 4:3-4, 4:6, 6:10, 6:30, 8:20, 16:12, 27:4, 29:2-3, 29:12-17, 29:23-25, 30:25, 31, 32:1)

After reading these, I have developed a pretty good understanding of Job's life before the trials began, and there is one reoccurring theme. Job made a practice of helping people.

His life reminds me of a story I heard recently of Eagles quarterback, Carson Wentz.

Carson was drafted by the Philadelphia Eagles out of North Dakota State in the first round of the 2016 draft. Sadly, around that same time, a young man by the name of Lukas Kusters was diagnosed with stage four stomach cancer.

Growing up, Lukas loved football and played until he got sick. His favorite team: the Philadelphia Eagles.

He had Eagles decorations all over his hospital room, and when his nurse found out about Lukas' infatuation with Carson Wentz, she made some connections with the Eagles' organization to share his story. A few calls were made, and, three days later, Lukas was on I-76 headed to meet Carson Wentz.

Lukas got to participate with the Eagles practice, eat lunch with the team, and was given a personal tour of the entire facility by Mr. Wentz. At the end of their day together, Lukas gave Carson a bracelet with his nickname from Pee Wee football inscribed over the top—The Dutch Destroyer.

Before Lukas left, he ran up to Mr. Wentz, looked him in the eyes, and hugged his waist. Carson took a knee, and with tears filling his eyes, they embraced. Cancer had already taken his voice, so Lukas was limited to expressing his emotions.

Months later, in an interview, Carson was asked about that goodbye and said, "It's an honor to know Lukas and be able to play a part in his life." Wiping the tears from his eyes, Carson concluded by saying, "Though Lukas couldn't talk, in that moment, he said everything he needed to say. Life is about more than football."

Thirteen days after his visit, on June 12, 2017, Lukas passed away. He was buried in a Carson Wentz football jersey.

As the next season rolled around, Lukas's family gathered around the television to watch their first Eagles' game since his passing. To their shock, they saw on the wrist of the young Eagles' quarterback, the bracelet that Lukas had given him all those months before. Lukas's mom burst into tears because of the compassion that Carson had for her little boy.[vii]

I think it was remarkable that Carson was able to provide hope and happiness in a story that had none. We, too, have the possibility of bringing happiness, comfort, peace, shelter, wisdom, and joy to the people walking through difficulty. Especially when we are in a space to offer help.

Just like Noah, Daniel, and Job, what we do during the noonday will prepare us for the suffering that comes during the night. If we are making habits as Noah did, praying as Daniel did, and helping others as Job did, we will train for the trial we are not yet in.[viii]

Don't get noonday and sunburnt!

CHAPTER TWELVE

ROOM OF OUR PAST

I wanted the past to be the last thing I wrote about because death, relationships, vulnerability, mental illness, and broken dreams are often the catalysts of a past that we are not proud of.

Your life is only one experience away from changing everything.

This chapter is for those who do not see God anywhere. Who are not sure if they believe there is a God. Who are not sure if life is worth living. Or if anyone even cares for them, and to be honest, the only thing they are confident in right now is that they are hurting. In this chapter, we want to ask the question "Can God redeem your life?"

> Your life is only one experience away from changing everything.

Maybe you are reading this at the bottom. Maybe you drank yourself down into a hole of darkness—but there is good news. We have a savior who, in a tomb of darkness, rose again, and he is willing to meet you at the bottom of whatever crevice you find yourself in, lift you out of the darkness, over his shoulder, and carry you into a new life.

Now that may sound like preacher talk, and maybe it is, but I know that God is the same today, yesterday, and forever. And the same God who rescued Daniel from the mouth of the lion, Noah from the flood, Job from himself, Shadrack, Meshack, and Abednego from the fire, Paul from the prison, Joseph from his brothers, and Jesus from the pit of death, is the same God that we serve. And he can and he will do the same thing for you—if you want that.

Jesus was walking beside the pool of Bethesda and noticed a man who had been sick for thirty-eight years. The pool was known for healing the first person who jumped in.

Jesus turned to the man and asked, "Do you want to be healed?"

The man answered, "I can't, sir. For every time I try to get into the pool when the bubbles come, someone else gets in ahead of me." Jesus replied to that man, "Stand up, pick up your mat, and walk" (John 5:6-8, authors paraphrase).

Maybe that's you today? You have tried healing in every way but Jesus. You have run from him your entire life. You have tried to find healing in drugs, alcohol, sex, money, clothes, cars, bars, and everything in-between. But none of it has brought you any healing. Jesus is asking you today, right now, "Do you want to be healed?"

If that's you, I invite you in the quietness, or in the commotion around you, to pray. Ask God to do a healing in you in the next few moments that only he can do.

If you grew up going to church, you have heard the story of how Saul, a persecutor of Christians, became Paul, the builder of the Church. If you haven't, just picture Darth Vader picking up the Sith Lord and throwing him over the railing to save his son; ultimately turning him from the dark side of the force to the light.

Most of us know the story, but can God do in us what he did for Paul? Can we have a restart, a reboot, or even a redo at life?

I certainly did not write this book for people with a clean past. I want those of you who have wandered off and somehow wandered your way into reading this book to know that your story is not finished. But to do that, first, you must discover where your past became perverse.

Some of you can point to a specific day that your life fell apart. For others, it was a slow fade, and now you find yourself at the bottom. Either way, getting to the root of the cause will help you in moving forward. We all have pasts, but no two pasts are the same.

Perhaps, your biggest meltdowns came from something you couldn't control. Maybe a doctor called with the news, "stage four cancer." Or maybe your company had to downsize, and you were collateral damage. Either way, it was nobody's fault; it was just **life's uncontrollable circumstances**.

Or maybe your downfall came at the **hands of someone else**. Maybe you entered into a relationship of hurt and distrust. A parent told you they would never leave or abandon you only for them to walk out the door when things became difficult. No matter the scenario, somewhere in your past, others have come against you in a way that changed the course of your life.

Some of you have nobody to blame but **yourself**. It was your fault. You sent yourself down into the hole. You sent the pictures. You were given a decision to make, and you chose wrongly. You cheated. You drove drunk. You lied. It was all your fault. Often times, life's uncontrollable circumstances lead to bad decisions on your part.

Stop for a second and ask yourself, "Where did my past go wrong?" Can you think of a specific event? Maybe a person? Maybe a place? Do you have an idea?

Girl with the Pearl Earring

The first time I laid my eyes on Catherine Moultrie was my senior year at Mississippi College in a communications class. She sat right beside me, and it was all I could do not to stare.

This is so random, but she reminded me of *The Girl with the Pearl Earring*. Every day she wore these pearl stud earrings to class with her wet hair in a bun. She resembles the portrait to a T. So one day, I got the gumption to tell her so:

"You look like a girl in a famous painting," I said. "I believe the painting is called *Girl with the Pearl Earring*."

She looked at me strange, then replied, "I don't guess I've seen that painting before."

I laughed, pulled out my phone, and showed her a picture. She nodded, "Yeah, I guess I do kind of look like her, huh."

Through the years, that painting has always been special to us, so this past Valentine's Day, I decided to buy her a replica of it. The only problem was that it was uber expensive—several hundred dollars in fact. Money which I did not have.

While I was searching around on the internet to find a cheaper replica, I ran into some information that explained why this painting was so expensive. The headband of the girl in the painting is made of the most expensive pigment known to man, ultramarine blue. The color can only be made from lapis lazuli, which is worth more than its weight in gold. Honestly!

Unlike most other gem materials, lapis lazuli is not a mineral. Instead, it is a rock composed of several different minerals. To transform this rock into paint, the minerals are thrown into a crucible, quenched, finely grounded, and then washed.[i]

I found out that not only was this portrait painted in ultramarine blue, but paintings such as *The Starry Night* by Van Gogh and *The Virgin in Prayer* by Sassoferrato were painted with the exact same pigment. In fact, almost every time that Mary was depicted in the Renaissance Age, lapis lazuli was used to represent her outfit.

I just love how Louie Giglio, one of the great communicators of our day, describes this phenomenon. He just nails it when he says:

"Lapis lazuli is called royal blue, not because it's the royals of the dynasties of the worlds who got painted in it, but because Mary, the mother of Jesus, and the angels were painted in it. It was a precious color reserved for the very best, and it came from the pulverizing and the crushing of a valuable gem that had to be mined up out of the ground."[ii]

This pigment went from a colossal bust to a royal blue. And so can your life. Yes, the cross is stained in crimson red, but God took what looked like a colossal bust and turned it into something beautiful, and he will do the same for you.

FROM THE PRISON TO THE PALACE

Just a glance into the life of Joseph resizes everything for us. From the time he turned fourteen until the time he was in his mid to late thirties, his life was a complete wipeout. He had been sold into slavery, thrown into prison, and forgotten about: all the while, doing nothing wrong.

In other words, his life was a colossal bust. But God elevated Joseph to second in command in all of Egypt. In one day, he went from the prison to the palace. God used Joseph, not in spite of his past, but through it. His past did not hinder him from fulfilling everything God wanted for him. Nor did it come off the back of bad decisions rationed by him. Instead, his past prepared him for his future.

It's possible that your setbacks in life are actually a setup for what God wants to do through you. God does not want to take your past and change it. Instead, he wants to take your past and redeem it for his kingdom's sake and for his name's sake. Take, for example, Moses. God didn't find Moses in the middle of nowhere and say to him, "Okay Moses. Now that I found you, I want to change everything about you."

No.

Instead, he took someone who grew up in the house of Pharaoh, only to make a complete mess of his opportunity, and redeemed him. God didn't fix Moses' problems, but he used his past—the good and the bad—to deliver his people to the promised land. And God wants to do the same thing with you.

Three Ultra Important Truths to Let into Our Room

We must have some turn-around moments in life if we want to onboard with the hope that God has in store for us. The first turn-around moment for us to believe is this; **the circumstances of our past do not circumvent God** from accomplishing his purposes for our lives.[iii] Let me say it another way; no matter your situation, God will not be sidestepped by any setback in your life. His plans will not be thwarted. Take Jonah, for example. Running from God, on a boat, sleeping in the dungeon, God found him and sent him by fish to minister to the people of Nineveh. We all have a past.

- Destruction
- Decay
- Depression
- Hatred
- Pain
- Brokenness
- Bullying
- Envy
- Regret

But no matter your past, your circumstances do not circumvent God. Look at Romans 8:28 (NIV), "We know that in all things God works for the good of those who love him and are called according to his purposes."

The first part is enough for us right now, "in all things, God works." You might not see God working in all things or know how God is working out everything for his glory and our good. But know that in all things, God works.

I love what Joseph *didn't* say when he was escorted out of prison:

- He didn't give a twenty-minute briefing to answer, "the problem of evil."
- He didn't explain all his philosophical or theological discoveries.
- He didn't explain why he was thrown into the prison and forgotten about in the first place— probably because he didn't know.
- He didn't question God asking him to explain why the last eighteen years of his life had been a complete train wreck.

Instead, what he said was, "He brought me to this position so I could save the lives of many people" (Genesis 50:20, NLT). Joseph knew that the circumstance could not interrupt God's plan.

The second big turning point that we all must have is understanding that **God is consistent through the inconsistent.** The Bible says it this way, "Jesus Christ is the same yesterday, today, and forever" (Hebrews 13:8, NLT).

In other words, the same God that used Thomas the doubter, Peter the denier, Paul the persecutor, Moses the murder, Abraham the aged, and even Rahab the prostitute, is the same God who is there for us through all the inconsistencies in our lives.[iv]

In one of the best sermons ever given, Judah Smith says this:

"Your greatest challenge is not your disciple, your devotion, your focus. Your greatest challenge is believing the Gospel.

"Could it be?

"That there's a God with a love so scandalous. So wide. So deep. So vast. So high. So expansive. So welcoming. So inclusive. 'Let me have your sin, son!' 'Okay.'

"And I give him my sin. And I stand in this empty space of forgiveness and acceptance, while Jesus walks off to the cross that I deserve.

"I see 'um, I see 'um walking up to the post to be whipped, as I stand a free man. All the attention is turned now, and I feel the love of God saying, 'Go son; live your life. I'll pay the price.' Where did we get off thinking that we were gonna, set ourselves free?

> God is consistent through the inconsistent.

"It's still Jesus! It'll always be Jesus! It'll never stop being the power of Jesus! If

his blood is sufficient for your salvation, his blood is sufficient to sustain you through every challenge and every sin and every temptation!
"JESUS.
"IS.
"ENOUGH."ᵛ

The first time I heard that sermon, I was in tears.

Jesus can take whatever inconsistencies that are present in your past, and consistently carry you through, forgive, and move you towards his purpose and his plan for your life.

UNPACKING OUR BAGGAGE

Many times, the baggage from our past gets carried all the way up to the present and into our future. We pull up the U-Haul trailer, fill it up with our past regrets, and drive around with a bus full of baggage. It comes to lunch with us. It goes to the gym with us. It shows itself in our marriage. It is present at the soccer game. No matter where we go or how far we run, our past is always with us. And until we stop to unpack our room filled with our past failures, mistakes, regrets, and pains at the feet of the cross, we will never stop living in the past.

The last truth still required to onboard is that **you have been found out yet forgiven.**

When I was growing up, I loved to fish. My dad has always been a great fisherman, and one of my oldest memories happened at a golf course where my mother, father, and I were fishing. We would always play a game to see who could catch more fish between us, and this time, I caught more than they did combined: two to zero ☺.

This confidence sparked in my seven-year-old brain the idea that my calling in life was to become a professional fisherman. Therefore, I did what every guy does who has a great idea: go to Academy Sports and buy everything I needed to make my dream a reality. The only problem was my Academy Sports and Outdoors was also known as the backyard shed.

I went and stole all my dad's fishing stuff, took it to my room, and placed it under my bed. (As you can tell, I was not a very smart kid. I mean what was I going to tell dad the next time we were out on the water? "Yeah dad, I rode my bike down to the store and bought the exact baits you use with monopoly money.")

As soon as I got the baits and fishing poles under my bed, Mom came in and knew immediately something was up. I was not then, and am not now, a good liar, so I quickly told her that I had taken all of Dad's fishing gear.

She then told me the words that every child hates to hear: "Just wait until your father gets home and hears about this."

You have been found out yet forgiven.

I began to cry uncontrollably, "Mom, please don't tell Dad. Please don't tell Dad." I begged her for hours. To my surprise, she finally said, "Drake, if you will quit crying, I won't tell your dad."

"You promise?" I questioned.

"Yes Drake, just replace the baits and go to your room."

I didn't believe her, so as soon as Dad walked through the front door, I never left his side. He ate; I ate. He got a shower; I sat outside the door. He went to the store; I road with him.

However, Mom never told my father.

Because of my repentance, Mom chose to forgive and not punish me in the way I deserved. I had been found out, yet forgiven, and that is exactly what God is saying to us.

Many times, we hide from God. We sometimes even run from God, but he wants to tell you and me today that there is no sin that he does not know about. In the history of forever, God has not one time said, "Ohhhhh. You did what now?" "I didn't know you did things like that." "Nobody ever told me."

There is nothing you can do that goes unseen by God.

Now that might scare you a little bit, but it shouldn't. Because God still loves you in spite of all your sin. There is no need to hide from God like Adam and Eve. Nor is there a reason to run from God's mercy as Jonah did. Instead, when we come to God in repentance from our past and our sins, God is faithful and just to forgive. Where sin abounds, grace abounds all the more (Romans 5:20, NIV)

We have built the foundation for the room of our past in saying that our circumstances will not circumvent God. This takes much **faith** to believe. We have also said that God is consistent through our inconsistence in the cross of Jesus Christ. This is the great **hope** of the Christian belief. Lastly, we learned that we have been found out, yet forgiven. And the only way this can happen is by **love**. These three—faith, hope, and love—only converge at one place in history: the cross. And it is these three truths that will launch us out of our past and into the glorious future God has in store for us… "And now these three remain: faith, hope, and love. But the greatest of these is love" (1 Corinthians 13:13, NIV).

A Cyst from the Savior

When Catherine and I returned home after being in the hospital all day, frankly we were just happy to be alive. Catherine began to share with me the story from her perspective, and while she was recounting it, she began to cry while describing how happy she felt in the moment the doctor told her that she didn't have any brain bleeds. (Could you imagine in one moment, thinking you were about to die, and the next, having hope that you are going to be okay?)

About a year later, this story resurfaced, and I remember thinking to myself, *"At birth, Catherine's life was in danger, but nobody knew it; not the doctors, not her family, nobody. But although nobody could see God working, he was saving Catherine's life from her very first breath."*

God's hand of protection in Catherine's past went unseen for twenty years, until she got in a car with me, and went soaring through the air like Dukes of Hazard—revealing that from birth she has had spinal fluid capsulated in her cranial cavity.

She very easily could have died as a baby, but God was watching over her. She didn't know it then. She didn't know that God was working in her past. She didn't know as a young child singing, "He got the little bitty baby, in his hands," that God actually held her in his hands from the time she was born until now. But every time she sang that song, God could have been thinking, *"Amen. Amen. You have no idea how present I have been in your past. I have held you in my hands every step of the way."*

In **your** life, you might not see God working. Many times, you won't ever know he is there. You won't see every blessing God has dealt to you. But I can guarantee you this; God is working in your past and for your good; whether you see it or are blind to it. Just trust in him and worship every step of the way.

I love you!

And I'm praying for you!

CHAPTER THIRTEEN

THE PROPOSAL

I hope you have enjoyed this book, and I hope it has been a blessing to your life. A few years ago, singer-songwriter Caitlin Crosby introduced an organization called The Giving Keys.

The idea of a Giving Key is to keep it through difficult moments in life to encourage strength, hope, courage, and fearlessness. Then, when your trying times have passed, give the key to someone else going through something similar as a testimony to pay it forward. It will let them know that you made it through, and they can, too.

In a similar manner, after reading the book *Unashamed* by Lecrae a few years ago, I gave it to one of my best friends, Kelon Elley, whose story I knew related to Lecrae's in many different areas. I gave Kelon the book in hopes that it would help in his journey through a fatherless adolescence.

Thinking about this method birthed in me the idea to do the same for *Midnight Worship*. I want to encourage you to keep this book for as long as you need it. Meditate on it. Read it when you need it. But when you make it through the midnight, give it to someone else who is going through their most difficult trial. Tell them the story of what midnight worship is all about and how you got through your most difficult road. Use wisdom and prayer to think of a person who could most benefit from your testimony and the words found within these pages. I pray that you will pay (or say) it forward.

I have told several stories within this book, but I hope you are okay with just one more. It comes from my personal diary. I try to keep a journal of thoughts that journey into my head so that I can look back one day and remember where I have been. I have never shared a journal entry with anyone before, so you are the first, but here it goes.

THE PROPOSAL

August 7th

8:58 P.M.- Well, I am getting ready to drive down to Birmingham to ask Catherine's parents for their permission to marry her. I am like, super nervous, but anyways, I'll keep you updated through the process. Chick-fil-A closes at ten, so gotta hurry to make it there in time. Can't drive four hours to Catherine's house on an empty stomach.

10:03 P.M.- Well, my GPS had me getting to Chick-fil-A at 9:57, so I rushed all the way here just to find out I forgot my wallet at the house. No chicken tonight!

Also, I have no idea how I am going to get home. My gas tank is on "E," and I only have $3.35 (which I found under my seat) to put gas in the tank. Hopefully it's enough to make it back to la casa. I plan on grabbing my wallet and getting back on the road. Wish me luck—I'll need it.

<u>10:43 P.M.</u>- I'm sitting in my car typing as I wait on Mom. She is the best mom ever; just saying. She drove thirty minutes at almost midnight to meet me with my wallet. #momgoals. Turns out $3.35 wasn't enough money to make it home. I still plan on driving to Catherine's, by the way. I should get there around 4:00 a.m.

Once I get my wallet, I'm going to buy a Mountain Dew! I'm pretty sleepy.

August 8th

<u>4:04 A.M.</u>- Well, I just pulled up to Catherine's house. She is coming out now to get me so I best be going. Planning on sleeping in late tomorrow and waiting to find the right time to ask her parents. I am a procrastinator, so if I know me, I'll wait until the last possible moment to ask.

<u>8:22 P.M.</u>- **I am so nervous right now.** Catherine, her sister, and all her friends have left the house to go play glow in the dark frisbee, which I didn't even know existed!

I can barely type because my hands won't quit shaking. I decided to stay back because now is going to be my most opportune moment to ask her parents with no one around. I didn't plan on asking them this early, so wish me luck. This could make for an awkward two days if they say "no." My apple watch says my heartrate is ninety-four beats per minute and getting faster. My stomach is already in knots. I'll let you know how our talk goes and until then, I'm going to try not to puke.

8:52 P.M.- So after giving myself a forty-five-minute pep talk in the shower, I finally came downstairs to talk with Catherine's parents. The only problem is no one can be found. I don't know where they are. I don't want to go barging in their bedroom, so I guess I will sit here for a little while and see what happens.

P.S. Beats per minute: 105!!

8:55 P.M.- Oh no, here comes Mama Carol. Yikes.

10:09 P.M.- I already know what you're thinking: "It's past 10:00. Did you and Catherine's parents really talk for an hour?"

Yes... We did.

Towards the latter part of our conversation, unfortunately before we could say a prayer, Catherine began knocking on the window. She came home from frisbee golf early to see if I was okay because I hadn't answered her texts in hours. *"Did y'all get to finish the conversation?"* you might ask. Yes. We used code to communicate. It was great.

Both her mom and dad SAID YES, so that is a huge relief and burden lifted off my shoulders. I could not be happier with how the conversation went. Well, maybe besides the fact that we got cut short, but they gave me some practical advice on marriage and managing finances. In return, I did my best to listen carefully without having a heart attack from the nerves and was just real, honest, and open with them about my intentions. All in all, it was a great talk, great night, and the beginning of a great proposal. Thanks be to God!

Now I have to get to bed. We have a 6 a.m. prayer service at Church of the Highlands tomorrow morning. I'll be back in touch soon though. I want to talk with her sister next and get her permission as well.

August 23rd

11:29 P.M.- So my last two weeks have consisted of nonstop ring shopping.

Did not know rings were so expensive! Literally thinking about going with a Ring Pop. I have been to every pawn shop, jewelry store, outlet mall, and online website that I can think of.

"Did you really look for her a ring at some pawn shop?"

Don't judge me. I'm a broke college student. I eat Little Caesars three times a week.

I never got the chance to talk to Elizabeth, Catherine's sister, to ask her for permission by the way. She is coming to help Catherine move in tomorrow, and I think it would be a wise idea and also a courteous gesture to speak with her in person—and to ask for any ideas on how to pop the question. I have no idea how I'm going to do that? Like how in the world am I going to ask Catherine to marry me? I have been thinking for two weeks, and I've gotten nowhere.

August 26th

2:49 P.M.- Mr. Phillip, Catherine's father, called me today and wants us to take pre-marital counseling. I'm not that big a fan of the idea with my packed schedule this fall semester, but he offered to pay for it, and after all, it can't hurt. I really respect her father, and he is one of the smartest men I know, so if he thinks it's a great idea, that's good enough for me. Not to mention, he is an all-around gentleman. Now I just gotta find some free time to schedule it in. *Hmmmmmm.*

August 30th

6:45 P.M.- Catherine's uber mad at me. She drove seventy-five miles to my house from school to surprise me with a visit. The only problem was when she walked inside, I was on the phone with THE JEWELER. What are the odds? So instead of being really excited to see her, I ran outside of the house with my phone saying, "Gotta go, gotta go, gotta go, gotta go" (I am so cool under pressure… not). I jumped on the four-wheeler and drove out to our barn. I called the jewelry store back and explained what happened.

"What are the odds of that?" the jeweler said.

"I know, right."

Laughing, we finished up the order. (I found Catherine a ring by the way. It is a small gold band with a ¾ carat oval diamond. I think she's really going to like it.)

I came back inside to a hornet's nest.

"I drove all the way up here for you to run outside when I walked through the door? I mean, who were you even talking to anyways?"

Pray for me! I might need it in these next few hours. Also, I still haven't asked Elizabeth yet. I told you I was a procrastinator.

October 23rd

<u>10:06 P.M.</u>- I have been writing the last few days, but my computer updated, and I lost all my unsaved files, so there's that. Also, it is Catherine's birthday today, soooooo "Happy Birthday, honey."

Just to catch you up to speed, Blake and I drove over to Birmingham to pick out the perfect place to propose. It took a lot of searching but we finally found it—a beautiful view overlooking the city at the top of Oak Mountain. It's perfect. The hike up the mountain is about an hour. But hey, maybe I can work it into my grand proposal speech as a metaphor or something: "Marriage is a journey! Lots of bumps and an uphill climb but the destination is beautiful."

Catherine's family and I talked later that week and decided November 2nd would be the best day to get everyone together for the big day. Her brother and his girlfriend are driving down from South Carolina, my parents are driving over from Mississippi, and her grandparents are going to attend as well.

November 1st

<u>7:48 P.M.</u>- Well y'all. It's the night before the proposal. I am getting a bit nervous working on my speech. This is what I got so far. "Dear Catherine." **That's it, lol.** I am having significant writer's block, but I'm sure inspiration will come sooner or later. Hopefully sooner than later.

I took pictures for the book cover today so that was cool. The same girl that did my book cover is taking our pictures tomorrow. She is awesome.

<u>11:42 P.M.</u>- Well. It has been four hours and I've done nothing but watch basketball and vibe in the hot tub listening to KB.

Still no speech. Soooooooooo, "Goodnight." Hopefully I will find the right words in the back of my eyelids.

November 2nd

<u>8:00 A.M.</u>- Today's the big day. Still no speech by the way, so I decided to go with a letter. Dad just walked in and gave me a pep-talk. More like words of wisdom than a pep-talk really, but I appreciate the advice. He also wants me to go absentee vote in a few minutes. One of the perks of living in the South I suppose. It's expected of you to do your citizen duty and vote.

Anyways, Clayton and Shelby, two of our best friends, will be here in a few minutes, and then we will depart to Birmingham.

Looking forward to an amazing day!!

THE PROPOSAL

10:07 A.M.- I FORGOT THE RING!!! The most important thing. I am such a goober. I'm about to turn around and go get it.

12:45 P.M.- We are stopped for lunch so I figured I could get some journaling in. Catherine tried to call me earlier today, but I couldn't bring myself to answer. After all, I knew she would ask what I was doing, and I didn't want to lie so I just ignored her call.

She has no idea we are coming up here by the way. Hopefully this Original Chicken Sandwich will give me some energy for the long hike up the mountain. I was reading earlier and it's a six-mile journey up to King's Chair.

2:32 P.M.- I think Shelby might pass out! Some young woman just handed us a map with the encouraging words, "Good luck with that hike!" as she handed it over. Low key, I think she doubts our ability. Can't say I blame her giving that we haven't hiked a day in our lives. But it's whatever. WE GOT THIS!

4:18 P.M.- This view is immaculate. Catherine is heading up here now with her sister and best friend. Meanwhile, I'm trying to find somewhere in the bushes to hide. (To Drew and Ty, or anyone else who understands this reference, "He's in the bushes!")

To my surprise, I am super calm. I thought I would be antsy. Honestly, I was more nervous to ask her to be my girlfriend than I am now, asking her to be my wife. Anyways, I won't be able to write again until the proposal so let's hope she says yes.

P.S. I got the letter written. I just finished writing it. I don't know if I will be able to make it through without crying.

Wish me luck!!

<u>5:15 P.M.</u>- SHE DID. SHE DID. SHE SAID YESSS! Well, she didn't actually say, "yes," she kind of just nodded her head crying—same difference.

We are on our way down the mountain right now. I'm pretty excited and also trying not to fall. Everybody is waiting on us so I got to hurry, but I want to share with you a couple of thoughts running through my mind: 1) I think Catherine already knew about the proposal because it didn't feel like she was surprised. However, I'm okay with that. Girls have a sixth sense anyways, so I kinda already figured as much. 2) I got through my letter. I got choked up at the beginning and a bit towards the end, but I got it all read. This is what I wrote:

Dear, Catherine. It's been a minute since I first saw you in communications class. From the moment I first met you, I knew it. I'm not sure what "it" was but you were different. You were sweet, considerate, kind, loving, gentle, patient, funny, humble, loved to laugh, loved my family, love me, and most importantly, you loved God. You put Christ first in a way that was and is genuine in nature. To that I say you live by the verse, "We love because he first loved us."

Life is a journey isn't it? Almost like your hike up here, its full of bumps that we didn't ask for or see coming. We will stumble, fall, and fail. That is part of living, but know that when you fall, I will be there to help you up. Not just me, but Christ in me, which is the hope of glory. Micah 7:8 says, "Do not gloat over me my enemies. For though I have fallen, I will rise." Every time we stumble together, we will rise also.

Uncertainty awaits us. The future can be thought out, anticipated, and prepared for, but never known. The Bible says it this way, "Man makes his own plans, but the LORD determines his steps." So I can't tell you what our future holds, and I can't tell you what life will look like, but I do know that I want to spend the rest of my life with you—chasing your goofy butt through the woods duck hunting, making jokes that nobody understands. More importantly, I want to spend my life walking after God and his desires with the one person he has made for me.

Catherine, will you marry me?

November 4th

3:38 P.M.- From the time I first wrote you driving over to Birmingham until now, a few things have happened: I went into debt, Catherine became my fiancée, and all the anticipation of the weekend is over. Yet the marriage planning is just beginning. Catherine and I haven't talked about the wedding yet. However, those talks will surely begin to creep into our conversations in the next couple of weeks until the final vow has been announced. Once we both say "I do" and the rings have been placed as a sign of commitment, we will finally walk down the aisle as husband and wife.

However, before we ever get to that moment, I will look Catherine in the eyes and say these few words, "I, Drake Nelson, take you, Catherine Moultrie, to be my lawfully wedded wife; to have and to hold, from this day forward, for better, for worse, for richer, for poorer, in sickness and in health, until death do us part." **And that is essentially what we are saying in this book.**

In sickness or in times of health. When I am satisfied. Or when I am in discontent. In death. Or in abundant joy. **I will worship you, God**, until, by death, I depart from this earth. And when that happens, I will step foot into eternity praising the one who is worthy of it all.

I will praise you, when I understand and when I am oblivious to your brushstrokes. When I agree with your purpose for my life. Or when I think I have no purpose in life. When my cup runneth over. Or when the bank account runs dry. **I will praise you.**

Midnight worship isn't a new idea. People have been saying it from the very beginning of time:

David - "Even though I walk through the valley of the shadow of death, I will fear no evil." "You will give me a song to sing in the night."

Job - "Even though he slay me, yet will I trust in him."

THE PROPOSAL

Micah - "Even though I have fallen, I will rise. Though I sit in darkness, the LORD will be my light."

Habakkuk - "Even though the fig trees have no blossoms, and there are no grapes on the vines; even though the olive crop fails, and the fields lie empty and barren; even though the flocks die in the fields, and the cattle barns are empty, yet **I will rejoice in the LORD!**

I want to leave you with one final verse in *Midnight Worship*. It comes from the book of Job:

"But no one says, 'Where is God my maker, who gives songs in the night' " (Job 35:10, NIV).

God will give you a song in your midnight! And when he does, sing it!

God Bless You!

"But no one says, 'Where is God my maker, who gives songs in the night.'"

CHAPTER ONE—GREATER THAN YOUR MIDNIGHT

i   Louie Giglio, Goliath Must Fall Winning the Battle Against Your Giants. (Thomas Nelson Inc, 2017).
ii   William Jordan, "Why the Mockingbird Sings : And Why at Night, When Most Birds Sleep?," Los Angeles Times, January 25, 1987, accessed August 31, 2019, https://www.latimes.com/archives/la-xpm-1987-01-25-tm-5613-story.html.
iii   Aseel, "What Is the Purpose of Steel Reinforcement in a Concrete Floor Slab?," Quara, last modified March 21, 2017, accessed March 26, 2019, https://www.quora.com/What-is-the-purpose-of-steel-reinforcement-in-a-concrete-floor-slab.
iv   Louie Giglio, The Air I Breathe: Worship as a Way of Life, 2017.
v   Giglio, Goliath Must Fall Winning the Battle Against Your Giants.
vi   This section is influenced a lot by Louie Giglio's sermon at the Lift Tour, 2018. It can be found at https://www.youtube.com/watch?v=ZihrWebHpcc.

CHAPTER TWO—MIDNIGHT IN PHILIPPI

i   Louie Giglio, Goliath Must Fall Winning the Battle Against Your Giants. (Thomas Nelson Inc, 2017).
ii   Forecast and Support Office NWS Analyze, "NWS Analyze, Forecast and Support Office," accessed January 10, 2019, http://www.nws.noaa.gov/os/hazstats.shtml.
iii   Giglio, Goliath Must Fall Winning the Battle Against Your Giants.

CHAPTER THREE—THE KEY TO MIDNIGHT

i   Levi Lusko, Through the Eyes of a Lion (Nashville: W Publishing Group, 2015).

CHAPTER FOUR—ROOM OF DEATH

i   Levi Lusko, Through the Eyes of a Lion (Nashville: W Publishing Group, 2015).
ii   Joseph Solomon, "A Shadow of A Doubt (Spoken Word)," last modified August 1, 2014, accessed January 19, 2019, https://www.youtube.com/watch?v=QeY8lndPs-dE.
iii   Lysa TerKeurst, It's Not Supposed to Be This Way: Finding Unexpected Strength When Disappointments Leave You Shattered (Nashville: Thomas Nelson, 2018).
iv   Christine Caine, Unexpected Study Guide: Leave Fear Behind, Move Forward in Faith, Embrace the Adventure, Study Guide edition. (Grand Rapids, Michigan: Zondervan, 2018).
v   Louie Giglio, "How Great Is Our God," YouTube, last modified September 26, 2012, https://www.youtube.com/watch?v=atUGBua2AzE.

CHAPTER FIVE—GYM OF DREAMS

i   Levi Lusko, Through the Eyes of a Lion (Nashville: W Publishing Group, 2015).
ii   Lysa TerKeurst, It's Not Supposed to Be This Way: Finding Unexpected Strength When Disappointments Leave You Shattered (Nashville: Thomas Nelson, 2018).
iii   Thomas Lake, "THE SHOT THAT SAVED LIVES," Vault, last modified March 2009, accessed October 24, 2019, https://www.si.com/vault/2009/03/16/105787321/the-shot-that-saved-lives.
iv   Steven Furtick, The Danger Of A Dream (North Carolina, 2019), accessed December 2, 2019, https://www.youtube.com/watch?v=RH0hAEOYKsI.

CHAPTER SIX—A DIFFERENT KIND OF EARTHQUAKE

i   "Moment Magnitude Scale," Wikipedia, November 3, 2018, accessed November 21, 2018, https://en.wikipedia.org/w/index.php?title=Moment_magnitude_scale&oldid=867101396.

END NOTES

CHAPTER SEVEN—ROOM OF MENTAL HEALTH—OR NOT-SO-MENTAL-HEALTH
i   Matt Haig, Reasons to Stay Alive, Main edition. (New York, N.Y.: Conongate Books, 2001).
ii Ibid.
iii Michael Devitt, "CDC Data Show U.S. Life Expectancy Continues to Decline," accessed December 2, 2019, https://www.aafp.org/news/health-of-the-public/20181210lifeexpectdrop.html.
iv Matt Haig, Notes on a Nervous Planet (New York, New York: Penguin Books, 2019).
v   These symptoms were taken from Matt Haig is his book, Reasons to Stay Alive.
vi Haig, Reasons to Stay Alive.
vii Levi Lusko, Through the Eyes of a Lion (Nashville: W Publishing Group, 2015).
viii Haig, Reasons to Stay Alive.

CHAPTER EIGHT—ROOM OF VULNERABILITY
i   Brene Brown, Dare to Lead: Brave Work. Tough Conversations. Whole Hearts. (London: Ebury Publishing, 2018).
ii   Ibid.
iii Lecrae Moore, Unashamed. (Nashville, TN: B & H Pub Group, 2016).
iv   Brown, Dare to Lead.
v   Ibid.
vi   Ibid.
vii This section relies heavily on Brene Brown's book, Dare to Lead.
viii Ibid.
ix   Ibid.
x   Lesley Unniversity, "Perception Is Reality: The Looking-Glass Self," accessed September 6, 2019, https://lesley.edu/article/perception-is-reality-the-looking-glass-self#targetText=The%20Looking%2DGlass%20Self,they%20believe%20others%20view%20them.&targetText=According%20to%20Self%2C%20Symbols%2C%20%26,but%20rather%20within%20social%20settings.
xi   Louie Giglio, "FATHER'S DAY - Seven Words That Can Change Everything - YouTube," Passion City Church, last modified June 18, 2019, accessed September 13, 2019, https://www.youtube.com/watch?v=7HSKDC8MjCw.
xii Brown, Dare to Lead.
xiii Swipe Right: Life, Death, Sex, and Romance., 2017.
xiv Brown, Dare to Lead.
xv   Louie Giglio, I Am Not But I Know I Am: Welcome to the Story of God (Sisters, Or: Multnomah, 2005).

CHAPTER NINE—FULL MOON CHRISTIAN
i   Craige Lewis, "'Keep Your $10': 'Christian' Rapper Andy Mineo Mocks Fans, Defends Profanity Use – EX Ministries," February 16, 2016, accessed June 19, 2019, http://www.exministries.com/keep-your-10-christian-rapper-andy-mineo-mocks-fans-defends-profanity-use/.
ii "Americans Are Spending More Time Listening To Music Than Ever Before," last modified November 9, 2017, accessed June 19, 2019, https://www.forbes.com/sites/hughmcintyre/2017/11/09/americans-are-spending-more-time-listening-to-music-than-ever-before/#4caaaedd2f7f.

CHAPTER TEN—ROOM OF RELATIONSHIPS

i   C. S. Lewis, The Problem of Pain, [The Christian Challenge Series] (London: The Centenary Press, 1943).
ii   Brene Brown, Dare to Lead: Brave Work. Tough Conversations. Whole Hearts. (London: Ebury Publishing, 2018).
iii   Lysa TerKeurst, It's Not Supposed to Be This Way: Finding Unexpected Strength When Disappointments Leave You Shattered (Nashville: Thomas Nelson, 2018).
iv   Susan Piver, The Wisdom of a Broken Heart: An Uncommon Guide to Healing, Insight, and Love, Edition Unstated edition. (New York: Atria Books, 2009).
v   Ibid.
vi   Swipe Right: Life, Death, Sex, and Romance., 2017.
vii   C. S Lewis, The Four Loves (San Francisco: HarperOne, 2017), accessed January 26, 2019, https://www.worldcat.org/title/four-loves/oclc/972735486&referer=brief_results.
viii   Swipe Right.
ix   Louie Giglio, "Pulling Together or Drifting Apart," Passion City Church, last modified 2015, accessed January 25, 2019, https://www.youtube.com/watch?v=Qh-JqI91lm3Y.
x   Nicole Fisher, "How Much Time Americans Spend In Front Of Screens Will Terrify You," Forbes, last modified January 24, 2019, accessed September 13, 2019, https://www.forbes.com/sites/nicolefisher/2019/01/24/how-much-time-americans-spend-in-front-of-screens-will-terrify-you/#6b5a13141c67.
xi   Brene Brown, Dare to Lead: Brave Work. Tough Conversations. Whole Hearts. (London: Ebury Publishing, 2018).

CHAPTER ELEVEN—NOONDAY AND SUNBURNT

i   Levi Lusko, Through the Eyes of a Lion (Nashville: W Publishing Group, 2015).
ii   Danika Worthington, "Full-Sized Replica of Noah's Ark Built by Tiny Colorado Company," Denver Post, last modified August 5, 2016, accessed November 27, 2018, https://www.denverpost.com/2016/07/31/noahs-ark-replica-ark-encounter-kentucky-builder/.
iii   Quentin Fottrel, "People Spend Most of Their Waking Hours Staring at Screens," MarketWatch, last modified August 4, 2018, accessed January 19, 2019, https://www.marketwatch.com/story/people-are-spending-most-of-their-waking-hours-staring-at-screens-2018-08-01.
iv   Malcolm Gladwell and Joosr, A Joosr Guide to Outliers by Malcolm Gladwell: The Story of Success (United Kingdom: Clitheroe, 2015).
v   Andre Agassi, Open, 1 edition. (Indiana: Vintage, 2009).
vi   Ravi K Zacharias and Vince Vitale, Why Suffering?: Finding Meaning and Comfort When Life Doesn't Make Sense (New York, N.Y: FaithWords, 2015).
vii   Tim Mcmanus, "Carson Wentz Grants Final Wish to 'Dutch Destroyer,'" ESPN, last modified October 22, 2017, accessed January 19, 2019, http://www.espn.com/blog/philadelphia-eagles/post/_/id/22568/carson-wentz-the-dutch-destroyer-and-a-dream-come-true.
viii   Lusko, Through the Eyes of a Lion.

END NOTES

CHAPTER TWELVE—ROOM OR OUR PAST
i "Lapis Lazuli (Afghanistan) Pigment," Natural Pigments, accessed February 4, 2019, https://www.naturalpigments.com/lapis-lazuli-afghanistan-pigment.html.
ii Louie Giglio, "Passion City Church Podcast," The Comeback, n.d., accessed February 4, 2019, https://itunes.apple.com/us/podcast/passion-city-church-podcast/id400379025?mt=2.
iii Ibid.
iv This chapter draws heavily from a sermon given by Louie Giglio at Passion City Church which can be found at https://itunes.apple.com/us/podcast/passion-city-church-podcast/id400379025?mt=2.
v Judah Smith, Jesus Is Loving Barabbas (Seattle, Washington: The City Church, 2016), accessed September 9, 2019, https://www.youtube.com/watch?v=XBbV-0jn_Cxo.

MW

END NOTES

MW

CPSIA information can be obtained
at www.ICGtesting.com
Printed in the USA
LVHW111953240221
679844LV00023B/607/J